I REMAIN YOUR LOVING WIFE LIZZIE

I REMAIN YOUR LOVING WIFE LIZZIE
Letters in a skip 1917-1919

Transcribed, edited and
with an introduction by
ROGER JEFFERIES

GREENWICH EXCHANGE
LONDON

Greenwich Exchange, London

First published in Great Britain in 2017
All rights reserved

I Remain Your Loving Wife Lizzie
© Roger Jefferies 2017

Printed and bound by www.imprintdigital.com
Typesetting and layout by Jude Keen Ltd, London
Tel: 020 8355 4541

Cover design: December Publications 07951 511275

Greenwich Exchange Website: www.greenex.co.uk

Cataloguing in Publication Data is available
from the British Library.

ISBN: 978-1-910996-15-7

ACKNOWLEDGEMENTS

Annie Hume-Almeida without whose quick action Lizzie's letters would have been sent to the tip with the rest of the skip's contents.

Graham Caldwell in Melbourne, Australia, whose main interest is military genealogy and who generously researched Tom Green's military records and provided them freely for inclusion with Lizzie's letters.

Helen Tovey, Editor of 'Family Tree' magazine, who published my article on these letters and encouraged me to find a publisher for them.

Richmond Writers' Circle for their encouragement and support.

Alison Williams for her editing skill.

James Hodgson and his team at Greenwich Exchange.

The London Borough of Southwark for permission to use the photograph of Ossory Road.

CONTENTS

Introduction

∾

IN THE SUMMER OF 2014 I was given a collection of letters, family papers and photographs by a friend. She had found them in a skip outside a property in Broadstairs, Kent. The property was being cleared after its owner, an elderly spinster, died without leaving any family. The documents were in no order and my friend knew nothing of the dead woman. Somewhat reluctantly I tried to make some sense of the material. There was no guarantee that anything of any interest would emerge. But there was a bundle of neatly folded letters which made me curious and, on cursory examination, they seemed to date from the First World War. Before I could read them properly I had to find out who had written them and to whom. Very quickly I became engrossed by the research required to identify the family and the correspondents. After sifting the papers and making searches myself in the relevant registers I knew who they were. Lizzie and Tom Green were married in July 1913 in the Southwark registry office (London). He was twenty-one and she twenty-three. He was the son of a journeyman sugar boiler and she the daughter of a railway porter. His occupation was given as an insurance agent and hers as a corset maker's canvasser. In May 1914 they had a son, also Tom but known as Tommy. By then Tom senior was working as a sewing-machine agent and, from the papers, the firm was Singer. He remained employed by them until he enlisted in 1916. Lizzie carried on working for the corset-maker throughout the war with her 'book' of customers on whom she called in the Old Kent Road area of south-east London.

During the war and after it, until Tom was discharged from the army, Lizzie and Tommy lived in a rented house, 74 Ossory Road, off the Old Kent Road, not far from Bermondsey and the London docks. She took in lodgers.

The family details provide a context for the correspondence, the bundle of letters. These are an engaging discovery, a peep-show into an ordinary woman's life, a woman separated from her husband by the war, enduring it, bringing up her small son, keeping up her job, surviving the daily events which bore down on her. Over one hundred letters survive, written by Lizzie to her husband. Only two of his could be found.

After enlistment in 1916, Tom was sent to India in the Autumn of 1917. He was a gunner in the RFA (Royal Field Artillery). Her letters begin just before his departure. They cease at the point of his embarkation to return in late 1919. He was discharged in January 1920.

We learn very little about Tom's experiences in India. His address was Mhow, Central India; but why he was there and what he was doing never becomes clear from her letters. The letters are not primarily about him. They are about Lizzie and her life. They are full of love and loneliness, almost written as a stream of consciousness as things come into her mind. But they are not great literature. They are often banal, whining, full of despair. There is plenty of cliché and most begin with a ritual greeting, such as, *"Just a line hoping to find you in the pink of health as it leaves us at present dear…"*, and often conclude, *"Hear [here] I must leave you I remain your loving wife Lizzie kisses from Tommy."* They are badly spelled; she has recurring difficulties with certain words: *hear* for *here, alful* for *awful, now* for *know.* There is little punctuation, the text flows with only a sudden capital letter to show that a new subject is starting. And *dear* appears frequently as if she is speaking to him.

The rhythm of the writing is often like speech. You can hear her. She sometimes doesn't know what to write and then suddenly she remembers something to say. She writes about her love for him, the pain of being apart and her longing for him to be back with her.

It may be a surprise that there is no patriotism, nothing at all jingoistic. She blames the king for the war: *"Well dear I have had about enough of this being on my own you ask me in your letter how I like it not at all and the sooner this war is over the better it will be for us both as it is the most rottenest life one could have being on the own as we are dear through no fault of our own only for the greed of the King that is all, what I want to know is this why should all men suffer and wives and children be parted from one another and not only that being killed at the same time just to suit the King's greed that is all and I cannot see the use of it at all can you dear…"* (April 21 1918).

Otherwise Lizzie makes no reference to the causes of the war, whether it is just or for a purpose. She shows only some brief excitement when the Germans are being defeated in the field in mid-1918. There is no national pride, no reference to being British. The war to her is murder in France, and, for her and Tom, an outside event which they have to endure. She refers to God only as some superior power, but there is no mention of religion or to her attending church or chapel.

She writes frequently about Tommy's development, his pranks, how others admire him, his cheerfulness, his views about his father being in India. He has some ill-health, problems with his chest and nose; he survives flu. He comes across as lively, a 'handful'.

"By the way dear you ought to see young Tom he is a lad I can tell you I have bought him a cap and he is throwing it up in the kitchen at the present moment saying lets sling a bomb at the germans, he is a right customer I can tell you he is getting quite tall and has [as] fat as ever dear, since I have had his nose and throat done he seems fine in his health dear no cold at the chest like he used to have I think it was worth having done" (April 20 1918).

"Young Tommy is a brick he take no notice of the raids, and he plays take cover, called Goodbyee and the kiddies sing a dittie to it and Tommy know it he sing all day long, this is it goodbye don't cryee 5-20 Gotha in the skyee when the maroon go off, should a bomb drop near, we is Goodbyee..." (June 25 1918).

"I cannot help smiling at him he is a nock-out I can tell you, he tell me that the airplane is going to fetch you home and drop you in the passage all I hope you bo[u]nce as I afriad [afraid] you will get slightly brosed [bruised] he is telling everybody about it and that you are going to buy him a little sister never mind he his [is] getting a fine boy dear and you will be surprised to see him I know Well dear I now close hoping you are quite well" (January 18 1919).

Lizzie is not sentimental; what she shows is the ebb and flow of daily living. She is, at one level, a feisty woman able to stand up for herself, but at another, she is vulnerable, a prey to despair and depression.

Lizzie describes the bombing raids in London, some very near Ossory Road, the advent of rationing, the price of food and clothes, the strikes in 1919. She has disputes with her lodgers, and the landlord. She has a big falling out with Tom's sister Carrie, who was keeping a boarding house in Worthing. She loses her brother in France; the wife of a friend is knocked down by a motor van in the Old Kent

Road and dies. She records the deaths factually; she is sorry for the children who survive but having recorded the events she does not linger over them. The flu grips London and kills many. She has two attacks herself but survives. She has a dispute with the Post Office over a broken parcel Tom has sent from India, but he sends her ornaments, a ring and silk. She has work done on her teeth. She wonders where they might live after the war and always she works at her 'book', saving the money in the Post Office Savings Bank and faithfully reporting to him the accumulating sum. She gets an increased allowance as a soldier's wife but carefully omits to tell the authorities she has a job. Above all, she takes up the cudgels in 1919, long after the armistice, to get Tom sent home and enlists Singers in her campaign.

She also talks in her letters about their physical relationship; how she remembers the cuddles they used to have and then she touches on more intimate things.

On May 10 1918 she writes: *"You ask about Tommy little sister well by the time you come home I shall be a maid and we shall have to start afresh I shall not mind so long as you don't want me to find the hole and another thing don't wrisetl [wrestle] with me like you did first go off, I expect it got out of control at time the only thing is to give it a wack and keep it quiet for a time dear so take great care of it and fetch it home safe and sound and good looking and bare [bear] in mind what I am saying."*

Later the same month she says, *"I do love you so, and you know it is true love dear and no spruce about it, I often feel I* have not been as I should be to you but it has been for our own good as I have only got the one child to look after when if we had been silly there might have been 3 or 4 children instead Tommy is off hand now and I can earn a shilling where I should have been hampered with more, never mind when you come home I will make it up to you dear, I won't care about what becomes of me then dear, here I close hoping you are quite well I remain your loving wife." (May 23)

On December 3 1918 she writes: "…*never mind so long as you keep it to yourself I expect by this time it is getting more than you can manage, but you tuck it in your trousers and then it will fade away, I expect I shall have to go through it when you come home but never mind I shall stick up for myself don't worry…*"

On December 26 she says, "*I don't think it will be long before we are together again then you will have to mind your p,a,q, [Ps and Qs] I can tell you no making babies as soon as you are home as I shall be getting wild, be like Mr Asquith wait and see keep on waiting and seeing that's the best dear, I suppose you dream of us and think of us a lot, I do you dear I often dream you are in bed with me to cuddle me nothing nasty just cuddling me so tight that I could not breathe at times dear, I often get wild when I wake up and find it['s] only a dream but never mind I hope it will happen in reality before long dear, only the waiting is so weary dear, one get so sick at times but is a long lane that has not got a turning for us both dear with God's will and everything is [? plotted] out in life for all so we must be patient and then we will have all in good time at God's will…"*

In her letters she takes up the theme of whether they might have more children when Tom comes home. Tommy would like a sister, and Tom is evidently writing to her about the possibility. She is characteristically forthright.

> May 26 1918:
> *"…in your letter dear I notice you spoke of our children I hope you wont go in for stock when you come home as I am not made for a lot of kiddies…"*
> In her letter of June 25 she explains: *"Well dear with regards to six or eight kiddies I don't think it matters I should very much like to have a little girl and Tommy would be off hand so I think it would be very nice dear and as you [k]now I always did like girls, but it is rather a funny thing to write about dear but I am quite cold minded about it and I really mean it I daresay you will smile when you read this, but it just what I have got in my mind dear, I said when you was home I should not like any more, but that was because I used to think of the time I had, now I feel much stronger I should not mind, never mind if go on talking like this I shall make you think you are at home and your mouth might water, but don't forget it must be a girl or I shall cancel the contract…"*

Lizzie and Tom had one more child, a daughter, in 1923. The letters give the impression that Lizzie was not afraid of being argumentative. Early on she has a dispute over her new teeth; her row with her sister-in-law Carrie meant that they were estranged well into 1919; she evicts her lodgers when they refuse to pay the rent because of a leak in the kitchen. She pursues the Post Office when a parcel of presents sent from India is broken. It also seems that she is on distant terms with some of her other relatives; she implies she is the subject of envy as Tom is in India and she has a job and some money. Perhaps she was not altogether easy-going. At the same time she is thrifty. She is very conscious of the cost of items of food and clothing which she often reports; she is hard-working and continues throughout the war and afterwards at her corset-maker. She reports to Tom about the bank account, (in the Post Office). By July 1919 there is £170 in the account, (at present day values about £7000).

Tom's last letter to her from India survives, though incomplete. It was written as he was about to embark on his return towards the end of 1919. It has a surprising tone.

"Well darling I don't know what you think about it dear but at last we are to get together after over two years. This is not so much as some others have had to put up with dear as they will have been away from their homes 4 or 5 years. I daresay I will have altered a great deal darling in ways appearance and manner of thought but I don't think my ordinary nature has altered much dear. But I hope all changes in me (and

*they will show very clear in you sharp eyes) will be for
the better. I think they are dear, and changes in
yourself dear will they be for the better if they are
I am lucky and shall glorify in them but if they are for
the worse I shall shut my eyes to them and remember
that you are a darling and much better than myself in
any case. For your bad points to me dear are only
surface and superficial but your goodnesses are deep
and everlasting, loyal and strong faithful and loving-
that is quite good enough in one woman; a perfect
thing is insipid dear… Well I close my last letter from
India here darling, I hope to be with you in nine or
ten days after you get this letter.*

So goodbye for a little while darling

*From your loving old mate
Tom"*

These letters are one-dimensional; there was no epiphany.
Lizzie's life was ordinary. There were momentous events
occurring in the world. There were deaths from bombing,
from flu, a famine in India, and overwhelmingly constant
reminders of battle and death in Flanders. But for Lizzie
and any individual living through those times at home, all
that could be grasped was the struggle for each immediate
day, in the street, at work, in the family. There was no bigger
picture for them.

Accounts of the First World War naturally focus on its causes, its conduct, its military strategies, and the suffering of combatants and the mounting casualties. Lizzie's letters remind us that these experiences were understood in their totality by very few while they happened. For her and others like her, the war meant separation, loneliness, hardship, fear, a daily struggle to live.

As it turned out there were no immediate personal losses for Lizzie and Tom. There was just a steady, monotonous and sometimes alarming grind, with nothing but their letters to remind them who they were and that they were lovers, until at last they were reunited and could start their lives again. That was as much a story for hundreds of thousands in that war as was fighting, death and mourning for others.

Barnes   *Roger Jefferies*
August 2015

Notes

⁓

The original letters and photographs

IN TRANSCRIBING THE LETTERS I HAVE endeavoured to capture the writing as it is, with spelling errors and lack of punctuation. I have supplied some corrections in square brackets, but generally the transcription follows the original layout and text.

The dating of the letters was problematic. Lizzie does not add the year and, in some cases, does not provide a month. I have been able to provide a year for each letter from the context and references in the text, for example, to Tommy's age, or their wedding anniversary, or the length of time since Tom's enlistment. Where no month is written, I have had to guess the month from the flow of events recorded in the dated letters. In the event I hope that I have been able to place all the letters in a broadly correct date order.

The letters are almost a dialogue, but to a modern reader used to instant e-mail responses the time for mail to go to and from India must have caused them some difficulty. Lizzie sometimes repeats herself in successive letters and has obviously forgotten what she previously wrote. Letters arrived for them sometimes in batches. Tom asks her questions to which she replies but there is a delay and he asks her again. He sends her money and it does not arrive and she has to ask again. The effect is similar to that of the gaps which used to be common in conversations in international phone calls.

The photographs among the papers are all unidentified. I have been unable to pinpoint a photograph of either Tommy or Eileen, his sister. I believe the photographs reproduced are of Lizzie and Tom, because the prints were mounted and kept together with the letters.

Tom Green's War Record

When I had finished preparing this text, 'Family Tree' magazine published an article about these letters in the December 2015 issue. At that point it appeared that no records existed to fill in Tom's war service.

Graham Caldwell, a subscriber to the magazine in Australia, read my article and was intrigued by my inability to find traces of Tom's war service. He wrote to me. He is a military history researcher and freely offered me the results of his entirely voluntary research into Tom's war service. I am very grateful to him and have included his complete report at Appendix 1.

Context

LIZZIE'S LETTERS WERE WRITTEN BETWEEN 1917 and mid-1919.

After Tom's conscription in 1916, the letters begin with the news of his posting to India in 1917, then continue during his service there, the armistice, and Tom's return and eventual demobilisation at the beginning of 1920. Lizzie's civilian life was less affected by the course of the military conflict overseas than by the immediate impact of major events at home.

This note gives a brief account of the background to some of the things which are reflected in her letters.

Conscription

Britain had not had conscripted military forces in peacetime, unlike Prussia and Germany. When the war came in 1914 Britain relied on volunteers to augment and replace the regular pre-war forces. And some 2.5 million enlisted. By the end of 1915 heavy losses and a fall-off in volunteers obliged the government to consider some form of compulsion. At first a statutory requirement was introduced for all men and women between the ages of sixteen and sixty-five to register their name and occupation and inviting men of military age to attest their willingness to serve. Then early in 1916 compulsory military service was introduced with significant exemptions including married men, but the latter was removed in May 1916. Conscription continued until March 1920.

Tom Green's attestation and then conscription are noted in Appendix 2.

Bombing

Germany began air-raids using Zeppelins in a campaign authorised by the Kaiser early in 1915, though initially London was excluded. He then agreed to attacks on the London docks, though initially they had little success. Damage was, however, caused to a number of coastal towns. Attacks continued against London but often failed due to bad weather or mechanical failures. Sporadic damage was caused in a haphazard rather than strategic way and largely in the suburbs. Defensive measures against the raiders were largely ineffective at that point. Although little strategic damage was done to the military effort, panic and alarm were widespread and the government had to take steps to divert resources and improve defence with artillery and airplanes.

Some raiders got through and a bombing raid took place over Bermondsey, Rotherhithe and New Cross in September 1915, and later attacks reached central London. During 1916 new types of Zeppelin were tried out but bad weather and further mechanical failure meant many raids were unsuccessful, though bombs were dropped in Greenwich and South East London as well as in other parts of the country. Aerial defences began to be improved and there were some successes against individual Zeppelin raiders.

The first aircraft (Gothas) were deployed in the spring of 1917. Air-raids caused little strategic damage but did kill civilians. The early Gotha raids were in daylight but the Germans began to suffer losses and, by the end of 1917, night-time bombing began and London received heavier attacks. The raids continued until mid-1918, but British airmen had increasing success against German aircraft.

Total deaths from all air raids were some fourteen hundred, of which over six hundred were in London. While these figures pale into relative insignificance compared with the death toll in the Second World War, at the time this was an entirely new form of warfare in which it seemed as if ordinary people were also targeted. The effect on morale was enormous. Makeshift shelters had to be devised, and 300,000 people took refuge in the Underground during night raids.

'Black-outs' were introduced gradually by law but on a local basis, at first in coastal areas and then in areas thought liable to air-raids. The restrictions meant reduced lighting at night and heavy curtains to ensure no light escaped.

Rudimentary warning systems were introduced during 1917 by firing maroons. In London, they were fired from fire stations or police stations accompanied by policemen touring areas on foot or cycle displaying 'Take Cover' placards, while the 'All Clear' was signified by whistles and further placards.

Food shortages and rationing

Britain was substantially dependent on imported food. German U-boat attacks on shipping, with unrestricted warfare from January 1917, meant that large tonnages of merchant shipping were being sunk. By the end of 1916, over two million tons of vessels had perished. No general system of food rationing was in place. There had been initial panic buying in 1914 and that began again during 1917. Generally, throughout the war there were shortages, often local, and as a result endless queuing was a common experience. Prices also rose. There was unrest in 1917, mainly caused by the problems of food shortages and cost.

The government began to intervene. A Food Controller was appointed and the Ministry of Food started to regulate the price of most foodstuffs and, in 1917, began to establish control over supplies. Local food rationing was introduced in December 1917 for sugar, butter and margarine, and meat from February 1918. A national rationing scheme was introduced in July 1918. Rationing continued after the armistice and butter remained on ration until 1920.

The Spanish Flu

This world-wide pandemic struck the UK in early 1918 reaching London by June. It had little to do in fact with

Spain, and was thought to have been spread by soldiers returning from the trenches. There were three waves and the effect was devastating. In London alone, between September and December 1918 there were twelve thousand deaths. More than two hundred and twenty-eight thousand people died in the UK. World-wide, more than fifty million succumbed. More people were killed than in the Black Death in the fourteenth century.

This flu was highly contagious. There was no cure and, with no antibiotics, no help for those who contracted pneumonia as a consequence. Simple precautions promoted included isolation, avoiding crowds, remaining in bed, and washing mouth and nose with soap to clear discharges. Theatres and other public buildings were closed; people wore masks in the street. Unfortunately, the armistice celebrations in the streets boosted a further wave of infections in November. And then as quickly as it had come, it faded away.

Not everyone died and for those who did not, recovery was swift. But the disease seemed to target not children nor the frail elderly, but the healthy in their twenties and thirties and forties.

Demobilisation

Notwithstanding the armistice in November 1918, conscription continued in place until 1920. At the end of hostilities in Europe there were almost 3.8 million men in the forces. Returning them to civilian life proved troublesome. The first scheme devised before the end of the war proposed to return first those most needed in industry. However, in practice that meant large numbers of those who had only recently been conscripted would be demobilised well ahead of those who had served much longer. There was a small mutiny, demonstrations and further public unrest at the perceived unfairness in 1919. Winston Churchill came back into the government at this point as Secretary of State for War and immediately set about reviewing the arrangements. Within days of taking office he produced a new scheme which was based on the length of service, age and the number of times a person had been wounded. This enabled a swift run-down to less than a million by the end of 1919, and by 1922 the armed forces numbered just over 230,000.

Industrial unrest

Although during the war there had been some periods of industrial action and a few strikes, very many fewer days were lost to strikes than in the period immediately preceding the war. That situation changed in 1919. Many disputes erupted, and although the government feared revolutionary fervour sweeping across from Germany and Russia, in fact the disputes were about pay and conditions, and sometimes about the scale and pace of demobilisation. Working hours had been cut after the armistice, prices had risen and workers were no longer prepared to accept the restraints of the war economy. In addition, there was widespread resentment at 'profiteering' from the war.

There was a small army mutiny in Folkestone and a naval one in Milford Haven. There was a notable police strike in August 1918 and another in July 1919. Engineering workers went on strike in Glasgow. A prolonged dispute with miners and railway workers resulted in a rail strike later in 1919. Working days lost rose from nearly six million in 1918 to nearly thirty-five million in 1919.

1917

∾

NOTE: TOM GREEN, LIZZIE'S HUSBAND JOINED up in 1916. There are no letters from that period though it is possible to deduce from some remarks in her 1917 letters that they had seen each other on his leaves. It is difficult to place the 1917 letters as nearly all are undated. However, from the context it appears that they were written towards the end of 1917 when Tom was finally posted, not to France as the first letter suggests, but to India. The date of his departure is not known but his arrival is recorded in her first letter in January 1918.

74 Ossory Rd
Old Kent Rd

[undated] [?1917]

Dearie
Just a line in answer to your letter dear I am so sorry to
hear that you are going to France so quick and pray God
will get this war to an end dear as it seems awful to know
you have got to go to such a horrible place you have
done no harm to anyone dear never mind hope for the
best and that God will bring you through safe dear and
you know I mean it with my heart dear. I am sending
you dental surgeries address and I want you to write a
stiff letter to them dear (Dukes 80 Rye Lane Peckham)
and try and help me with it as much as you can dear.
This conference sound alright dear don't you think so
and I wish with all my heart that it passes dear I do that
so as us 3 could be happy and comfortable again like we
used to be. Hear [here] I close dear as I shall lose the
post dear I remain your loving wife Lizzie.

74 Ossory Road
Old Kent Road

[undated] [?1917]

Dearest,
Just a line in answer to your letter dear which I received
this morning dear you seem to misunderstand me about
Mrs Irving, she came round on Friday but Nell said she
would stop dear, so Mrs Irving said she would come on
Monday so it all ended well and I collected £11-9-7 on
Saturday and Monday dear on Walworth — he seems to
be very pleased with me and he gave me 23 shilling dear
so that was good wasn't it.

Little Tommy has got [w]hooping cough I am sorry to
say who [how] I know the doctor said it was so. that is a
six week job but never mind, we shall get over it I
suppose. I have got Tommy up and he is at present
sitting in the front room with a nice fire dear. I want to
get him used to the air as I am going to take him to the
hospital as I think it best with that sort of thing now. I
want to know what hospital Singers subscribe to, as I
wanted to take him to the Surr[e]y Dis[pensary] but you
must have a letter for the place — that is the worst of it
and I have heard such good accounts of that place with
regard to [w]hooping cough. Dear, your bike has come
back to its home, I should have told you before as it
came home on Friday morning dear. I am sending you 2
shillings, cannot send you any more at present as I have
not been to the Post Office and shall not be able to go
until tomorrow dear as not being able to take Tommy
out and no one to look after him while I run this is very
funny I got Jack['s] Nell a skirt and she happened to
send me 2 shillings so that is who [how] I got hold of it

dear. Well hear [here] I close, hoping you are quite well as it leaves me at present.

I remain your loving wife, Lizzie

74 Ossory Road
Old Kent Road

[undated] [?1917]

Dearest
Just a line in answer to your Saturday letter dear I have
not been able to write before dear as we have had such a
time with these raids dear, this barrage of gun fire is
awful dear, it is quite unnerving dear, for 2 hours and a
half the guns were in process and the noise was
deafening to us and today we have had two sets today.
They were 20 miles off London this morning dear. I am
pleased to think you have not gone to India yet and I
don't seem to think that this war is going to last, as long
as people think this is the finishing up and please God it
is the case as not only the soldiers are suffering but the
mothers, wives and children too, but never mind. With
God's care we hope to pull through dear.

Hear [here] I close, hoping you are not being upset with
these raids

I remain your loving wife Lizzie

I have insured our place for £75 – the most I could
insure for dear

74 Ossory Road
Old Kent Rd

[undated] [?1917]

Dearie

Just a line in answer to your letter which I received this
morning dear I went to Rye Lane dear and they are
going to make me another lot they said that would see
my case throughly [thoroughly] through and I have got
to go up and have the set taken. Dearie you ask me to
give you luck well I wish with God['s] help that you get
the best of luck dear and as you know that has come
from the bottom of my heart dear. I am sorry to say that
Harry Bute has been wounded in the hand that is as far
as we know and my brother George they havant
[haven't] heard from him for a month I hope he is
alright as he as [has] had 1 or 2 [?] nowner except.
[? narrow escape]. All I hope is that you get out of it all
right for we have not done much wrong dear and it
seem[s] a shame that you should be parted from me as
you are dear never mind we have got a lot to make up
for by the time that you come home for good dear which
I hope will not be long dear and I know you feel the
same towards it. When I think of the time when you
have work so hard to get our home together and now
you are not hear [here] to enjoy it that is when I get so
full up and I expect you think the same way dear never
mind dear things will alter soon I hope and then we
wont half enjoy ourself dear hear [here] I close hoping
you are quite well I remain your loving wife Lizzie

Excuse spelling as I seem to have forgot a bit

74 Ossory Road
Old Kent Road

Undated – [?1917]

Dearie

Just a line in answer to your letter which I received I am
pleased to think you will be there for some time as it not
all honey for you to go out there dear as you know I
worry very much over you and it is awful to read the
paper about the war dear it is either some poor mother
or wife losing there sons or husband dear and it must be
shocking to know they have been killed dear mustn't it,
so the longer you stop there the better it will be for us
both dear. The weather is rotten here raining ever since
Sunday evening and no sign of it leaving off. I expect it is
the same there where you are dear. Do you think I had
better to write to Lingyards and ask them to send bike
home to me dear. I have been very unfortunate with
orders this week very quiet never mind things will wake
up after the holidays dear I have got next week off and
shall go and see one or two people I know have a couple
of days at Wood Green dear it will make a change dear
won't it. Hear [here] I close hoping you are not cross at
me not writing before dear and hoping you are keeping
quite well

I remain your loving wife
Lizzie

(love and kisses from little Tommy)

[illegible] Terrace
Lordship Lane
N17

[Undated] [?1917]

Dearest
Just a line [?] in answer to your letter by the way you
write you don't seem to have had [?] my letter you ought
to have received t[w]o since sunday night dear one I
wrote on sunday and one on tuesday dear you ask if I
have got my teeth dear I am sorry to say that I have not
had the money dear they are ready and they look very
nice but he wont let me have them until I have got all of
the money and the work has very quite [quiet] dear all
the people on my round more or less have gone away
out of these raids dear and it has hit me hard I have only
got 4 orders to come out this week dear, you know it has
upset everyone dear and people are feeling to[o] ill to
order stays but if these raids are only stop[ped] thing[s]
will go alright again which I hope will not be long dear
for this barrage of gun[s] seem[s] to be on top of us and
we seem to be deaf with the sound dear for it is not safe
to be out after the warning is given for they have got
guns up every street and it is just like a bombardment it
lasted 2 hours and a half on Monday night but last night
they did not come so we had a nights rest dear we have
not been to bed for nearly a fortnight dear has [as] they
have been giving us a time dear soon after 6o/c and then
we have had the firing up to turn eleven dear and have
not had the all clear order given to about one o'clock
never mind God has help us through the worst and keep
us safe and took care of us but is has been alful [awful]
dear you can bet. Dear if you could send that money
dear send it to Nells addresss but don't forget to register

letter so has [as] I shall get it safe dear and then I will
make it up to you dear hear [here] I close hoping that
you are quite well I remain your loving wife

Lizzie

Not Wood Green
Teynton Terrace
Lordship Lane
Tottenham N17

Undated [?1917]

Dearest
Many thanks for letter which I did not receive till
Tuseday dear owing to you putting the address Wood
Green dear never mind you will [k]now better the next
time you write I am having a change being down here I
don't think you had better take on as a layer dear as I
hear that is very dangerous dear do what you think for
the best as I don't understand it keep as well back as you
can dear for things are a bit hot with the guns now dear
in France God send you were not going out at all for it is
all a worrie dear when I hear what is happening out
there. I thank you very much for spoons dear but if you
are sending them let me have them by Friday dear as I
shall be going home Friday night as I start work
Saturday morning dear as usual. You ask after Jack well
he is quite well till now. I have been very much worry
dear at not hearing from you I thought perhaps you
were ill and could not write dear but never mind I was
pleased to get that letter dear. Nell and the children are
in the best of health and little Tommy is quite well I
myself am much better with regards to the bank that is
going alright dear. Hear [here] I close hoping to hear
from you soon dear don't forget after Friday I shall be at
home dear Hear [here] I close hoping you are quite well

I remain your loving wife Lizzie

12 Tynton Terrace
Lordship Lane
Tottenham
N.17

[undated] [1917]

Don't forget the address for the time being as if I go
home I shall get Nell to post letters on to me

Dearest
Just a line in answer to your letter dear. I am sorry to
hear that you are going on Sunday dear but I suppose
it can't be helped dear, what a pity you could not work
24 hours off, never mind dear we must hope for the
best dear.

I have got my teeth dear and they are so comfortable
dear and look lovely dear. I am sorry that I went to Rye
Lane dear, this set are a perfect set dear and I wish you
could see me with them in dear. I have slept in them all
night dear and I have eaten my dinner with them, in fact
I feel as if I have had them for months dear, they are
splendid dear. Never mind, I will have my photo taken
and it will give you a little idea what they look like dear.
I know you would be pleased to see them, they are
something like your own dear, they don't hurt me a bit
dear, he said "I have taken great pains with you, unlike
those other people and I want to please you, to try and
make it up to you." I think he is a fine old chap don't
you dear.

Tom I am sending you your watch on as I cannot get it
mended at all under 3 months as the shops all shut up at
five since we have had air raids, so I thought when you

get settled down a bit you could have it repaired dear as I wanted you to take it away with you as a little gift from me dear. I am sorry it is not in order but perhaps you will get over that little difficulty dear.

I don't think I want all that money dear as I don't want you to go away without any so as I have had the liabilities and I am giving a pound to Hicks out of that but that makes f3/14 to be made up for the dentist dear so if you can spare a little dear I shall be able to manage it I think dear as I have told you trade has been very quiet since you have been back from your life dear here.

I close trusting God to land you over safe dear and speed you back to me and baby.

I remain your loving wife,
Lizzie

74 Ossory Road
Old Kent Rd

20 Nov [1917]

Dearest
Just a line in answer to your most welcome letter as it
seem alful [awful] to have to wait for a letter so long
dear but never mind dear we must get use to that as we
will not be able to hear for one another so much but if
we write 1 letter over the other dear I think by what
I have been told we will be able to get a letter every week
I am sorry to hear you have had such a rough voyage
dear but trust to God and he will help you dear and also
me as I have been guarded though some alful [awful]
time dear with these raids as they have been very near
again but thank God we have been look after dear which
I hope we will be look after until we both meet again By
the way dear I have lost Mrs Barrett she moved 3 weeks
ago but I have let the rooms again and got two nice
people in they have got a little boy about 9 years old and
they seem very nice up to now dear and I hope they will
continued to be so By the way dear be careful how you
write you letters dear as the letter you sent was scratch
out with the censor I am sorry you will not be home this
Christmas but never mind you have got a lot of time to
make up when you come home for good dear. Bill
Pascoe his home on leave 14 days he look well, poor old
Bob has joined up and is at St Albans up to now I don't
[k]now if they will make him fit but he has got to stop
there for six week to see what can be done with him dear
I have had Tommy very queer with abscesses in the ear
the same kind of thing what he had when he was
younger and his cough is still very bad but if it was not
for him being so queer with [h]is cough and ear he was

alright but I don't suppose he will lose it just at present never mind it never rains unless it pores and I suppose it is a bit of rough luck but we will get over it dear. Your Carries has come home and look quite well so it has done he[r] the world of good. Well dear by the time you get this letter your birthday will be gone but I have not forgotten it dear it is this Sunday coming up so I wish you many happy returns of the day and hope the next time we will be able to spend it together dear if all goes well By the way dear Nell is expecting Jack home on leave dear the children are getting on great and are looking forward for there father to come home well dear I hope you keep in the best of health dear and also come home to me and little Tommy soon

I remain your loving wife
Lizzie

Love and kisses from Tommy

1918

∽

NOTE: TOM REMAINED IN INDIA THROUGH-
OUT 1918.

74 Ossory Rd
Old Kent Rd

Jan 18th [1918]

Dearest

Just a line in answer to your letters which I received
altogether one to say you were at India and the others to
say you were still on the ship dear, well I am pleased to
here [hear] you are landed alright and are very
comfortable dear as your letters read dear. You ask after
Jack well I am sorry to say dear he has been wounded in
both knees and brought to England to hospital in Wilts,
and George my brother is in hospital at bagdad
[Baghdad] with disintry [dysentery] but cannot get any
news from him only from the war office. Now your
brother George is in Italy and young bob has joined up
and is in England up till now. By the way we are having a
treat of our lives here we line up for tea sugar and milk
we line up for meat and bread we have had to register for
nearly everything in fact little Tommy want to [k]now if
we are going to have to line up for marengin
[margarine] every time we go out dear he thinks it is a
treat more than I myself do you can bear dear, we have
got a meatless day that is Tuesday I can tell you things
are very serious dear but I have manage to get what I
want up till now dear with a struggle never mind keep
on smiling riots every day on some shop or other if it is
not the maypole it [is] the Home & Coline [Colonial] &
the meat shop or the bread shop I don't think there
could ever been such time dear never mind we are to
have ¼ pound of margine [margarine] each to make up
for what we have been without for a fortnight dear never
mind as long as we get along alright we must put up
with it dear. You ask about my work well dear up to the

present things have been alright but there is going to be
a lot of differents [difference] for we have not got the
still [steel] as the government have claime[d] and Mr
Savage is only serving old custermers [customers] until
they brighten up dear so it is making a bit of diffrents
[difference] to me but I must not cry as things could be
worse dear. I say dear you must have had a terrible
voyage over dear but I am so glad you are safe dear I
have prayed every night dear for you dear that you
should land safe and God has answer[ed] my prayer and
with his help I do hope you will keep well and come
home soon dear as life is very blank without you dear
and I expect it is the same for you dear never mind there
is a lot to make up for when you return dear, you ask
after Carrie she is going on alright dear much better in
health than she has been more her old self and I am so
glad as she is such a good old stick dear. I have been
about my teeth dear and they are going to let me [k]now
in a week so as soon as I hear I will write to you dear I
told them I wanted my money returned I am going to
have a good try for it don't worry dear I shall do my best
I thank you for the postcard dear they are very nice and I
shall keep them dear as a little something from you dear
I should think it was a very nice place dear by the
postcard I expect you do look like babies [?]blowing
monkeys not babies. I suppose you find it a lot too far to
hop up on wednesday afternoon dear never mind I am
only pulling your leg I shall be pleased at having a photo
of yours because I want a pendant with your photo in
dear so I wait until you send me some don't forget
there['s] a pet I will have Tommy and myself taken dear
you will not know me with my teeth they are lovely and
people cannot tell the difference from my own dear I eat
with them and sleep in them and they are not a lot of
trouble and such a beautiful colour you must excuse

mistake dear as Tommy is worry worry all the time I am writing never mind he is a good kid and such a comfort to me dear hear [here] I close hoping you are in the best of health and all the good luck dear I remain your loving wife and baby

Lizzie and Tommy

74 Ossory Road
Old Kent Road

Undated [from context – early 1918]

Dearest
Just a line hoping to find you quite well as it leaves us
both at present I have had little Tommy with the chicken
pox but he has got over it all right and his [is] running
about again and quite well we have had the air raids
quite plentiful just lately but have come out quite safe
with the exception of the tail of our horses in the Front
room being knock off with the heavy gun fire never
mind all well that ends well dear. I am sorry to say that
our George is very ill with diserinthy [dysentery] and
has been sent to baddage [Baghdad] I trust by the next
time I write I shall be able to tell you he his [is] better
dear. Your George has been sent to Italy without having
any leave, you[r] Carrie is getting ever so much better
I have got some very bad new[s] our Jack has been
wounded in both knees, but he his [is] going on alright,
he has been sent to hospital at Wilts. I dare say you have
had my letter by now telling you about Mrs Barrett
moving dear I have got someone else in and they seem
very nice to[o] very friendly, there name is Bragg and
Mrs Bragg mind[s] Tommy for me why [while] I go to
work so it is much better than taking him into the cold,
but he look quite well with all of it. Mr Barrett is in
France he went on the day after Boxing Day and did not
have a leave after that day his first and last leave never
mind you had some fine leave didn't you dear and we
enjoyed ourself to[o] by the way how did you enjoy your
Christmas dear not [at] all if anything like myself it was
rotten dear I did so miss you it seemed as if I could not
bare it and I was glad when Thursday came and we went

to Bills they made us very comfortable but I miss you more than anything. Mr Lee asked for your address and I have given him the last one you sent me, Well dear what do you think of this war dear do you do you think it will soon be over everybody think this [? year] and I do hope it will be a peaceful year for us all everybody dear and than [then] I should expect to see you very much quicker dear, and I do ask God to help us be together again dear the same as we used to be and I [k]now you hope the same little Tommy is sending you a card one he pick out himself he said that was his daddy and that was his red suit so I had to put it in the letter dear has [as] he was waiting to put it in hear [here] I close hoping and wishing with all my heart we shall meet soon dear and also wishing you the best of health and good luck I remain your loving wife Lizzie

Love and kisses from your little Tommy
xxxxxxxxxxxxxxxxxx

74 Ossory Road
Old Kent Road

Jan 29th [1918]

Dearest
Just a line in answer to your lovely letters dear which I
received, one on Monday and the other on Wednesday I
am so pleased that you are quite well dear and going on
alright dear I thought you were getting at me when you
said you got a job in a picture palace, I suppose it makes
a change and you like music so of course if it comes to
you to play dear. I do not know if you have heard of the
air raids dear but we have had two and they have been
very bad 5 hours gunfire and a lot killed too but thank
God he took care of us and I hope he will as these raid
are alful [awful], and I expect you hear of them dear
never mind you must not worry as that does not make it
any better dear, little Tommy is very good when they are
hear [here] he said Mam that's the gun and there about
Mam, and when the guns are firing so heavy he said o
my earholes you Germans you cannot help laughing, he
is quite well dear and is getting quite tall and still keep
fat but is getting so pretty his face is round and a lovely
colour two cheeks like roses dear I [k]now you would be
proud of him if you saw him your Carrie thinks he get
on lovely and father said he is a fine boy; he is a dear kid
and he keeps things alive I should be dead without him
all he wants is a little sister and he cannot understand
why he cannot have one. I am sorry to say that George is
very ill with disintory [dysentery] and is in hospital in
Badad [Baghdad]. Hear [here] I close hoping you keep
well dear and will not be long before we are together
again dear I remain

Your loving wife Lizzie

74 Ossory Rd
Old Kent Rd

30/1/18

Dear

Just a line in answer to your letter I am glad you still love
me as you do, life sometimes seems so blank but when I
think how you love me it is much brighter dear I do
wish this war was over dear there would be something to
look forward for what with lining up for meat and this
and that I tell you we are seeing life dear never mind
keep on smiling and it will all come right in the end dear
I don't think the war can last much longer dear as
everybody is sick of it and what with the raids to[o]
things are getting very hot and when things have quieten
down you think it a treat to be alive dear but you must
not worry about us as you know I keep my head and do
the best I can under the curcanstance [circumstances]
dear. I think it is very kind of you to buy me a present
but you must not spend your money on me dear as you
might want it dear but you are so kind to me you always
was kind and that is why I miss you so dear never mind
there is a lot to make up for it dear and leve [?leave] to
us to make it. No doubt you are surprise to [k]now that
we have got food tickets ¼ lb of marg for each of us dear
and 2 meatless days a week but we are still going along
dear and things are not so bad under the curcs [circs.]
never mind it will not go on much longer dear the war
will so[on] be over and things will brighten up and then
we will have the old days back again

Hear [here] I close hoping you are well and wishing you
a happy time dear

I remain your loving wife Lizzie

74 Ossory Rd
Old Kent Road

Feb 11 1918

Dearest
Just a line in answer to your most kind and lovely letter
dear, I received parcel dear this morning. I am very
pleased with it and the glasses are handsome, the shawl
and scales are beautiful but I am sorry to say dear the
box has got broken, it is the lid dear and little Tommy's
bracelet has got broken but I think I shall be able to
mend them. They charged me 1/5 duty on the cigars, Do
you think I ought to write to the postmaster about it
dear? They are very pretty dear and I am most pleased
with them it must have cost you a lot to have bought
them but you are so good dear and I do hope you will
come back to me and baby safe. As when I think of you
and your kind ways it makes me so sad dear, never mind.
I will take great care of your presents and think most
kindly how me and the boy are in your thoughts night
and day dear I do hope your arm is getting better dear,
no chance of coming home for 48 hours with it this
time. Dearest I love those glasses and anything like them
I should like if you send anything again but you must
not distress yourself in any way as you want the money
to meet your little wants for yourself dear. If you want
any more money dear write and I will send you some
but don't send anything breakable again as it is such a
shame and it hurt my feelings when I opened it and
found it broken dear. I could have sat down and cried,
never mind as it is no fault of yours dear and it is so kind
of you to have sent them. I have not seen Kate and Grace
yet but they will be pleased with them when they get

them. I am taking 3 cigars to your dad and 3 to my dad as it is only fair you know.

I close hoping you will keep well and soon come home.

I remain your loving wife Lizzie
xxxxxxx
Xxxxxxxxx
from little Tommy

74 Ossory Rd
Old Kent Rd
[undated] [early1918]

Dearest,
Just a line to you to let you know we are still living, we
have had the biggest air raid dear and we have suffered
badly to[o] they have bombed Avondale Square and
Rotherhithe New Road and in fact all round, it was the
worst we have had 17 Gotha got to London so you may
guess how it was dear. I am thinking of moving right out
of London as my nerves will not put up with so many of
these raids dear I did not use to take much notice of
them but it is beginning to tell on me now, I feel very
much shaken up this time. I suppose it is being so near,
right at the top of the turning, you may guess it upset us
dear. I received your parcel dear and was very pleased
with it dear, it is very kind of you to think of us like that
but the way things are going on dear I wonder if you will
come home to us safe or if we will be spared to see you
dear these raids are most terrible. It is thundering and
lightning now and pouring with rain, we are having a
fine time I can assure you dear.

Hear [here] I close with the best of love, I remain your
loving wife
Lizzie

74 Ossory Road
Old Kent Rd

[undated] [early 1918]

Dearest,
Just a line to let you know that we are all quite safe after
the air raid dear, very near this time. 2 houses down in
Cobourg Road and Coopers in that road is in ruins dear
and one house in Odell Street down, 6 houses down in
Mina Road, just where we used to live, 10 people killed
outside the Dun Cow. Right from Surrey Square to the
Dun Cow and that turning round the back of the Dun
Cow dear there was 6 killed in one house so you see the
paper does not tell you right at all dear as it was such a
night on Wednesday, we were all so glad to see the
weather change dear as it poured with rain that
Wednesday night and we knew we were safe. I was so
glad that I was staying with Nell as I felt bad when it
started dear. I should have been worse dear if I had been
home but I have been home to see if things are alright
and you can rest contented that it is dear I was coming
through the city on Monday night when the raid was on,
in the bus I had a very nasty experience I give you my
word but thank God I landed at Nell's quite safe after
being shut up in the pub for 2 hours dear I am a little bit
shook up but I shall be alright dear after a couple of days
By the way dear address your letter hear [here] (Nell's
address) as I think I shall stop until I get little Tommy's
cough better dear.

Here I close wishing you the best of luck

PS (Don't feel upset dear but it is as well to [k]now what
to do)

I remain your loving wife Lizzie

PPS Don't forget to will that bank book over dear as
I have been told if anything bad happens there would be
trouble to get that money.

74 Ossory Road
Old Kent Road

Feb 19th [1918]

Dearest
Just a line to let you [k]now that we are going on alright
dear, We have been trouble[d] with the air raids again
Saturday Sunday and Monday nights and they have drop
there bombs very close to us but thank God we have
excaped [escaped] safe dear and I hope will continue to
do so dear no doubt you will get to hear about it so I
thought I would write dear and let you know we were
alright so as you will not worry dear they have done a lot
of damage these raids are most alful [awful] dear but
never mind we must grin and bear it dear they are very
nice people I have got in the house he is a most sensible
man and dos [does] not worry anyone and she is the
same it is quite a pleasure to have someone about you at
such times dear I can ashure [assure] you quite
difference between Mrs Barrett and these they make
cocoa while the raid is on and it seem[s] to buck you up
dear just as you used to be when you were at home dear.
I have wrote to the GPO about the parcel being damaged
and they answered the letter and I expect someone will
come down from the office dear I have put in for the
little box and Tommy braclets [bracelets] so if I hear I
will let you [k]now dear I do hope this war will be over
dear so as we are together again and these rotten air
raids are done with dear, I hope you are keeping quite
well under cover dear I now close hoping to find you in
the best of health as it leaves me and Tommy dear

I remain your loving wife Lizzie
xxxxxxxxxxxxxxxxx from Lizzie and Tommy

74 Ossory Road
Old Kent Rd

March 2nd [1918]

Dearest
Just a line in answer to your letters I received 3
altogether dear, you are a love to send me such a nice
present dear I cannot thank you enough dear to spend
your money on me like that dear the locket is beautiful
dear have not seen such a thing like it before dear I will
take great care of it dear and treasure it as it is so nice to
have someone that think[s] of you dear I often think
there is not anything to live for, if you did not love me as
you do dear, I am very luckey to have you love me as you
do dear, for there are many women have not got a man
to love them as you do dear and that is why I am doing
my best at home and keeping things straight for you as I
know will love me for it and make it up to me when you
come home dear which I hope will not be long dear,
Dearie do not think I am cross in any way but you
should not spend your money on me dear as it is so
gready [greedy] to take away from you dear I like them
very much and I am proud of you for thinking of me so
dear, but you must not drain yourself for the sake of me
dear, it is lovely to have a present sent from you dear and
it makes me so glad, I cannot hadly [hardly] beliveled
[believe] it hardly, I received the parcel but the lid of that
pretty box was broken and the bracelet dear I wrote to
postmaster General and they sent a postcard telling me
they would come and see me about it dear and when it is
settled I am going to give your dad those [?cigars] as my
people do not care if I am dead or alive dear and your
sister and father are very kind to me dear your carries
[Carrie] is very good and kind to me dear so I am going

to give her a scafe [scarf] dear which I [k]now she will
value very much more so than my sisters dear you don't
mind my altering my mind dear I noticed by your letters
you have been promoted dear from Gunner to
Bombadier I am pleased you are getting on alright dear
and keeping well dear as I hope you will continue to do
so dear I know you would like to know about the bank
dear, there is £40 up to now dear so we are going great
dear don't you think so dear I should have had more but
little Tommy has be[en] expensive with that cough but
he is alright in his self dear his cough is going great
nothing to worry at all dear, I am sorry I did not answer
this letter before but I have had little Tommy up the
hospital with his nose and throat but he is going along
alright dear. I have been to the post office about the
parcel I tole [told] you it has got broken the little box
and the braclet [bracelet] dear so I am waiting to hear
further dear, we have had another air raid dear, getting
quite used to them, but our barrage is grand the way
thay [they] are keeping them back is wonderful dear and
you would say so if you were here we get 20 minutes
warning we have [?maroons] go up it is a bit of a scar[e]
but the people take it fine they soon quiten [quieten]
thereselves down to it, I think you are very kind dear to
send those things but you must not spend your money
on me dear things are going great, but the pen has just
go[ne] wrong excuse spelling as I am a little bit out in
one or two words dear hear [here] I close hoping you are
quite well I remain your loving wife Lizzie

xxxxxxxxxxxxxxxx just a few from Tommy

74 Ossory Road
Old Kent Rd

March 15th [1918]

Dearest
Just a line in answer to your letters I have just received
dear one is dated 20/12/17 and the other is dated
29/12/17 I think they have been keep [kept] back for
something or other dear Well I have received parcel but
the box was broken and the bracelet to[o] dear, I have
been to the post office about it and they told me to write
and ask you the price of them and they will replace the
damage he said it was the custom house fault so will you
write and let me know as soon as possible dear so as I
can get it done with, dear I thought you would like to
know what was inside when I got the parcel, as it was
open dear there was 2 scarf 1 shaw[l] 6 wine glasses 6
cicages [?cigars] and a bracelet dear you must write and
let me know if I got all you sent dear, I also received the
necklace and I was very pleased with it dear it is very
good and very kind of you to send them to me dear but
you must not spend your money on me dear I know you
want to buy me little things dear but at the same time
you must look after yourself dear I read by your letters
that small pox have broken out I do hope and trust it is
not serious you ask me what I should like for my
birthday dear if I can choose it I should like a ring but
do not send it if you don't think I shall get it dear has
[as] I would much rather wait till you come home dear
then I should be shaw [sure] of it dear and a good many
more things to[o] I['m] thinking. I expect you was
surprise when you saw your name up for promotion but
be careful dear as stripes are not much good to anyone
dear I am pleased you had a nice Christmas dear it has

[is as] well they make you comfortable dear as so far from home as you chaps are it has [is as] well for you all dear I am pleased to tell you Tommy is much better I have had his nose and throat operated on an[d] he has pick up wonderful dear I have had him laid up with chicken pox but he is alright now dear, I am quite well in myself old sport you must not lay me up when you come home dear I am warning you old boy Old George has been very ill but his [he's] going on alright hear [here] I close hoping you are keeping well I remain your loving wife Lizzie

Excuse ink has [as] old Tom has knocked the bottle flying
74 Ossory Rd
Old Kent Rd

March 22nd [1918]

[incomplete]

Dearest
Just a line to thank you very much dear for your ring I
think it is so good of you dear you must love me very
much I can quite understand you it gets more than
enough to bear at times for me dear I have been very
down this week the more I think of you the more I love
you and the more it get[s] to[o] much to bear to be
parted like this dear do not think I am downhearted
dear because I am not I try and make the best of
everything, but your letters give me a jerk for I do try to
crush this rotten feeling dear but it is no good I love you
so much dear I cannot forget you I can always see you
when you were pleased with me and even when I made
you wild I can see you when you did not want to speak
to me and I coxed [coaxed] you to[o] dear I have had it
on with you dear but all a joke I did not mean anything
as you [k]now I have always thought such a lot of you
dear I love you with all my heart and sole [soul] dear I
would do anything to please you dear and also give
anything up to please you to[o]. I hope you do not think
I am to[o] pushing in this letter, but, you [k]now when I
have a line from you it a sort of well to be truthful about
it, it upsets me, and when I am waiting for a letter it is
the same I suppose it is because we love on[e] another so
much dear that we cannot get used to be parted and that
is the bottom of it all. You ask after Tommy he is in the
best of health now dear since I had his nose and throat

done it has been the making of him dear you would be please to see him he is getting so tall…

74 Ossory Road
Old Kent Rd

March 24 [1918]

Dearie
Just a line to let you know I got the parcel alright dear
with which I am more than please with dear the shoes
for Tommy are beautiful they fit him lovely dear My
shoe are very nice but they are not wide enough, what a
pity they are not a [?] durby front and then I think they
would fit as it is they dont dear I am very sorry about it,
as they are so soft dear and also very good I wonder if
you could get me a wider pair dear don't think I am
asking too much dear I also got Tommy hankys and
2 shilling he was very pleased with them dear I have got
photo as well they are very good dear of you have some
more done but have your face turning this way dear,
I was going to ask you to send me two of those
handkerchiefs dear as they are nice and big, and would
make nice [w]raps to[o] dear I hope you wont mind
dear, I think that brass work is nice you sent in the parcel
dear, it is very good of you to think of us dear, I have
been thinking today dear about you how kind you are to
us at home I do wish you were with us dear, the days
seem years lately dear waiting for you but never mind
dear hope on and you will be with us before long dear
I am looking forward for you dear I am very pleased
with the parcel but sorry the shoes dont fit dear well
dear must close as Tommy wants to go to bed

74 Ossory Rd
Old Kent Rd

[undated – but in reply to a letter 18/2/18-? March 1918]

Dearest
Just a line in answer to your letter which I received this
morning dated the 18/2/18 it is surprising who [how] I
feel just the same as you do dear don't [k]now what it is
I want but such a[n] aching feeling one could go mad at
times and the world seems blank dear all I know is I
want to be with you and I should not care a jot, never
mind we will live in a world of love when you come
home for good dear it is quite rotten I can tell you dear.
You seem to be having plenty of food out there by your
letters which I am pleased to hear, but you must not let
the feeling run you down has [as] you have not got
anyone out there to look after you if you are ill dear
which you be if you fret and that is what you are doing
dear I [know] the feeling only to[o] well dear never
mind dear all well that end well and there must be an
ending to it all I am sending you Georges address as I
think it is a little difference to the one I have just sent it
is

Gunner PG Golder
42583, 14th Battery
4thBrigade RFA
Mesopotamia Expeditionary Force (D)

I'm sorry you are not getting my letters dear as I have
wrote such a lot a [of] nice long letters to[o] which you
would like I [k]now, you ask after Tommy I should like
you to see him he always got his trousers torn he is all a
boy I can tell you he want to [k]now when this war will

be over and then you will come home and he will go to
work and you will say hear's [here's] young Tom coming
home to dinner he think you will be away long time
don't you think so never mind cheer up dear hear [here]
I close with fondest love and kisses I remain your Loving
wife Lizzie

[undated] [from context March 1918]
[incomplete]

I am sorry to say poor old Arthur has got to join up this
month March 28th he don't like it I can assure you, and
you will be surprised to know Mr Ward has been called
up he has gone 3 weeks ago and is at Bristol don't know
what lot he is in, our food hear [here] is very scarce dear
ration out with meat 1/3 per week for me and 71/2 per
week for Tommy ¼ lb of marg[arine] per week for us
both dear never mind we seem to manage alright I do
hope you are going on alright dear, I am so pleased with
your ring dear it's a beautiful dear every one has fell in
love with it dear and I cannot express my feeling enough
dear you know how I feel when you took me out and
bought me something I liked who [how] I used to love
you for it well that is just how I feel towards it dear you I
mean dear so when you come home you have got a lot to
have so get prepared for it dear and I expect you will be
making a mess of me (you know putting my figure[e]
out a bit .) I don't mind as long as I don't have twins as
they might keep us awake all night it will be like getting
married again wont it old sport never mind you wont
mind will you dear, I expect you are feeling gay after not
seeing me for 8 months dear never mind all the longer
the better dear and no doubt if you saw your son and the
games he gets up to you would have to laugh fancy he
has got the idea that you wont be home till the war is
over he say when the war is over my daddy is coming
home and he said to the boy next door why don't your
dad be a soldier and go out to the war like my dad and
then the war would be over tomorrow and my dad
would come home, fancy a kid having that in his mind,
to know if more men went the war would end sooner he
is a dear kid he think the world of you and he is looking

after me in his old tin pot way if your Carrie said
anything to him about me for she likes to hear his talk
he don't half tick her off and said I love my mum too big
ones, he [is] old fashion as the hill, he comes up to me
and said ain't you nice I don't [h]alf love you mum I say
no not down there, my neck as you [k]now he was fond
of putting his hand down, and he says no only round
your neck mum he is a dear kid, there is no mistake
about it, he saves you a place in bed against the wall, he
says my dad is going to sleep there when he comes home
Well dear I think that is all I have to say dear.

Hoping you are in the best of health I remain your
loving wife, Lizzie

PS I never send you kisses dear so I thought I would,
here are a few from Tommy and me dear
xxxxxxxxxxxxxxxxxxxx
xxxxxxxxxxxxxxxxxxxx

74 Ossory Rd
Old Kent Rd

March 27 [1918]

Dearest just a line in answer to your letters dear, well it
wants 2 days now to good Friday dear quite a
drifferrenet [different] day to what we have been used to
dear, I often think of the times we had together at
holidays dear when we lived at Darwin Street they were
the happiest times of our lives and we did not [k]now it
I often wish that I was back there and able to start all
over again dear how we used to have such good times
there dear it seems quite a pleasure to look back at them
never mind there is a silver lining to every dark cloud
dear and we have got a good time before us haven't we
dear I did not tell you that Mrs Bigham has little Tommy
of a day while I go out to work dear it is much better for
me and not far to go for him to[o]. Dearie I have just
thought that you are better off there you are as this big
push is alful [awful] and if you had been in France you
could have been in it and it would have been very
worrying to me now for I am sorry for those who are in
this battle dear I think of Flo['s] bill it is neck or nothing
out there now dear so it as well you are where you are
dear don't you think so dear no doubt you think you
have got a soppy old woman but I think such a lot of you
I cannot bear the thought of you being ill or hurt dear it
seem[s] alful [awful] to me I cant help it dear queer, I
cannot get Georges address dear only [k]now it is
Bagdad and he is much better he is out of the hospital
and at a resting home, but if I can get the address I will
send it on dear, the weather is very changeable one day
warm next day raining or very cold but taking it all
round we have had a decent winter dear today is the first

of April and it is rather cold to[o] but bright, I should
very much like to peep at you just to see if you are
getting very brown as I expect you look well and the
change has [as] well helps but never the less I expect you
think there is nothing like home never mind you wait till
you come home a baby first night, what, that cheacky
[cheeky] don't you think so, I [k]now that will make you
smile old sport, by the way your letter you get a bit
excited with this anatomy and physiology I should think
but I am glad you pass and alright dear it is something
to work for the other chap must have been ratty at you
getting the top never mind dear you earnt [earned] it
dear Dearie I have just found the address I had of
Georges it is in the letter dear

Hear [here] I close with fondest love and kisses I remain
your loving wife Lizzie

Kisses from little Tommy xxxx

74 Ossory Road
Old Kent Road

April 4th [1918]

Dearest
Just a line hoping you are quite well dear as it leaves us at
present. I am writing this letter dear as I am so full up I
don't know how to express myself I don't half love you
and I want to tell you so much the more I think of you
dear the more it seem to hang on I could not think I
should miss you so as I have, I know I should have miss
you but I thought it would have worn off but it is just as
fresh as ever dear in fact worse at times, dear do not
think I am downhearted dear it is not that but I love you
so dear I feel hurt at not being near you, as I feel that
there is nothing to take your place dear those nice times
we had together dear, I never really love you inti[until]l
we got married dear, well you know what I mean I did
love you but in a different way and you now seem as if it
is something I cannot live without dear, you are very
kind and thoughtful I suppose that is a lot to do with it
dear I do love you such a lot dear you may think
something has come over me so's to write to you like this
but if my heart and feelings could speak dear they would
say such a lot dear I can see you so much, a little Tommy
is growing up he is the model of you he is so kind and
good natured and so thoughtful too, you would be
surprised if you saw him, it is rather a long time since
you did so, I expect you are just the same dear must be
jolly rotten for you dear too but never mind I think you
far as ever dear, he plays take cover and all clear that is
for the air raids he gets a piece of paper and blows
through it all clear that is supposed to be the buglers he
drops bombs he gets lots of papers and go out to sell

them he calls out, 60 tons of bombs drop on the British I
don't think, he his [is] a lad you have to laugh at him, he
wakes up every morning and ask me if the Germans
came last night, and we get the real warning to take
cover he said 'Mum they're about' so cool you can't help
laughing. I have been under the doctor myself for
overstrain of nerves but I am going on alright now when
I was so queer little Tommy got a pillow and put it in the
armchair and told me to go to sleep and he would open
the door if anyone knock and he can reach the street
door so it just show you who [how] tall he is getting dear
he is a good kid to me and if he was older I feel shaw
[sure] he would be a great help to me dear he is a
wonderful kid his sence [sense] and nolage [knowledge]
is beautiful. He tell me you are in india and the war will
be over tomorrow and then my dad is coming home
mum he is quite shaw [sure] that you will not be home
till the war is over dear. Do not worry about me as I am
quite alright dear now the doctor said I was in time to
prevent being very ill, it was me nerves dear so nothing
serious that is why my spelling is rather bad dear I
cannot think of the word and when I do I cannot spell
them dear but I am ever so much better than I was 4
week ago dear so do not worry as you might be ill and
out there you have not got much hope of recovery I
could not stand it if you did not come back to us that is
all I hope to see you soon dear I now feel the same dear
we will never be parted again dear once we are reunited
it must be worst for you all them miles away dear but we
must live in hopes of seeing one another again and soon
dear hear [here] I close I remain you loving wife

Lizzie

74 Ossory Rd
Old Kent Rd

[undated] [Easter 1918]
[incomplete]

Dearest
Just a line hoping to find you in the pink of health as it
leaves us both at present it is Easter Monday today and I
thought you would like a line dear you ought to be
getting my letters alright now as I am writing 3 to 4 a
week dear but by the way the papers read our mails are
being sunk a great deal dear, I must thank you again for
that ring it is lovely and everybody said so you must let
me [k]now the cost of that box and braclet [bracelet] as
the post office are going to pay for it dear it['s] a shame
it got broken dear I am so sorry as it [is] such a nolvety
[novelty]. Well dear your son wants me to take him on
the round-abouts he his [is] a lad he says he [k]nows
where they are round the Peckham-park Rd by Perks
stores he nows [knows] what he his [is] talking about
alright leave it to him dear you would have to laugh at
him if you was hear [here]. By the way our work is
getting slack I expect I shall have to keep my eye open
for another job as he think[s] it will last another 3
months the Government has taken over our still [steel]
and it has given him a nasty smack in the eye, poor
Arthur has gone last Thursday his address is Pte A
Golder 53rd (y.s.Rifle Brigade) No 2 Company St James
End Northampton I thought you would like to write to
him he ask for your address I gave it him so I expect he
will write to you dear, Well you seem very comfortable
by your letters dear and I hope you will remain so it is
alful [awful] in France at the present time and I think
you are the best off where you are dear. I am fine in

myself now and I am pleased to[o] [it] is rotten when
you['re] queer and no one to look after me as you used
to when I was ...

74 Ossory Road
Old Kent Rd

April 17 [1918]

Dearest
Just a line hoping it will reach you same as I am so sorry
you have not received my letters I have written so nice
letter to you too. Now I want to now who [know how]
much that little box you sent me cost also the bracelet
to[o] as they got broke but the post office people are
going to repay the damage if you can let me no [know]
the cost, so let me know as soon as possible dear I got
the ring safe and I was very pleased with it dear and
everyone I have shown it to likes it. dear, it is most
uncommon now [no] doubt it cost you rather a lot dear
never mind it is very nice dear. We are having some
rotten weather hear [here], rain, rain all day long dear
gives you the pip if you have not already got it I can tell
you I can quite understand how you used to feel when
you was collecting and it rained I have the same feeling
myself dear never mind better days in store. You ask me
who [how] I like being on my own, to explain myself I
don't think I ever felt so misable [miserable] it is a rotten
life I don't like to tell you my real feelings towards it dear
its to[o] painful to think about never mind it cannot last
for ever dear it has got to come to an end sometime or
other and then it is our time to enjoy ourself and it must
come dear soom [some] day. You ask after the new
lodgers they seem very nice and also very comfortable
and quite [quiet] and the rent is share I am very satisfied
with them up to now dear if they keep as they are they
will be alright dear. Tommy is alright and has had his
haircut he like [looks] very smart he says so he is all the
boy I can tell you he will be 4 years old the end of next

month my it does not seem so long as that do it he will be a big boy when you come home I can tell you hear [here] I close hoping you are quite well I remain your loving wife

Lizzie

Fragment
[Spring 1918]

...are in the safest place dear for in France it is hell at the
present moment, bit rotten for those who are out there
dear, and the way you are getting on dear it sounds
alright dear and you deserve it as you are all a man could
be in fareness [fairness] and in every way, no doubt you
might feel flattered when you read this but you [k]now I
am proud of you and also mean it and when a woman
loves a man as I love you dear it is real no swank a man
ought to think he is the luck[i]est man on earth dear By
the way you ought to be getting my letters regular now
dear, I hear Jenny has written to you and Arthur so you
will have a few letters and you will not feel such a long
way off we have been very quite [quiet] of air raids lately
thank goodness you seem to get plenty of food out there
dear, we are very short, but not being many of us we rub
along alright but some people are suffering worse than
we are dear there are big familys that is the trouble dear
it will be a good job for everyone when it is all at an end
things might be a little better which I hope will not be
long as the poor fellows that are young under it alful
[awful] never mind it will come right in the end dear
hear [here] I close hoping and trust it will not be long
before you are home again and then you will be able to
make a fuss of me and cuddle and love me for ever dear
I remain your loving wife Lizzie

74 Ossory Road
Old Kent Rd

[undated] [spring 1918]

Dearest
Just a line to let you know that we are going on alright
dear. I have wrote to the Post Office about that parcel
you sent dear and now waiting for a reply dear. I am so
much upset about it but for the future dear do not send
anything breakable dear, I shall be sending you the
photo dear in a few weeks' time, I hope you are alright
dear in your health as it leaves us both at present dear. I
am pleased that you had a fete day as it makes a change
for you dear but if you have anything that you think is
going to break don't send it dear as they say they cannot
be responsible for the things at a long distance like India
dear. I am very pleased with the shawl dear, it is
beautiful, so lovely to wear I shall have to buy a
sideboard to show those glasses off dear. You don't know
how proud I am of them, they are lovely dear and I am
also very proud of you and I do love you so dear, at
times I cannot bear to think we are parted as we are dear,
miles and miles away dear. Do not send me more cigars
dear as that was the reason they opened the parcel and
pulled the silk out and at the same time broke that little
box and bracelet dear so I think you had better write and
make a claim dear, don't you? I am still going on alright
with my work dear and banking the money so if this war
is over soon we will have a bit to fall on dear. The real
thought of you coming home dear makes me feel happy
don't you think so dear? Lizzie Facer came and saw me
last week, her husband has had trench fever, been in
France 14 months. She has got such a nice girl too and
the kiddies are very nice, the people that are upstairs are

very nice and they think your parcel is lovely dear. Mrs Barrett has got a down-stairs across the road, I think she is alright. Mr Barrett is in France, been there since Christmas. Who do you think has married Miss Brooks dear, quite a surprise dear don't you think so. Little Tommy is getting a big boy and his little tongue is going 90 to the dozen. There is not a thing you can say without he has got it, he is pleased with his bracelet and so proud that you have sent it to him and the other things. He said they are lovely — funny old kid don't you think so. Your Carrie is going on alright dear, her health is coming back to her, now don't send anything you think will get broken dear as I don't want you to spend your money on me, but if I can get anything off the Post Office I will, leave it to me dear won't you.

I now close, hoping you are quite well.

I remain your loving wife Lizzie

Love from little Tommy and kisses
xxxxxxxxxxxxxxxxxxx
more if you were at home dear
xxxxxxxxxxxxxxxxxxx

PS I won't half make a fuss of you when I meet you dear, not a word about your age

74 Ossory Rd
Old Kent Rd

April 20th [1918]

Dearest
Just a line hoping to find you in the best of health as it
leaves us at present dear. Well dear you ought to be
getting quite a nice lot of letters as I am writing 3 to 4 a
week dear it is jolly rotten this waiting for letters as one
could be dead and not [k]now anything about it
couldn't you. Well dear we are having rough times of it
hear [here] with regards of food, we are rationed out
with meat that is ⅓ worth for me and 7½ for Tommy
that has to last us for a week with margine[margarine]
we have ¼ lb each and ½ lb of sugar and that has to last
us a week 1½ oz of tea a week but up till now bread is
not rationing jam and marmalade is very scarce so you
see we have to go very careful to make it do but we
manage alright up to now we have not had to go without
dear only we had to be sparing with all, and the food is
very dear but we manage. By the way dear you ought to
see young Tom he is a lad I can tell you I have bought
him a cap and he is throwing it up in the kitchen at the
present moment saying lets sling a bomb at the germans,
he is a right customer I can tell you he is getting quite
tall and has [as] fat as ever dear, since I have had his nose
and throat done he seems fine in his health dear no cold
at the chest like he used to have I think it was worth
having done, with regards to the new lodgers they are
alright up to now dear, my work is alright up till now
dear, but I afraid it will drop off shortly has [as] they
cannot get the steel to put in them dear never mind I
expect things will all come right dear Hear [here] I will
close with fond love and hugs and kisses Lizzie

74 Ossory Rd
Old Kent Rd

April 21st [1918]

Dearest
Just a line hoping you are getting letters by now dear,
Well dear I have had about enough of this being on my
own you ask me in your letter how I like it not at all and
the sooner this war is over the better it will be for us
both as it is the most rottenest life one could have being
on their own as we are dear though no fault of our own
only for the greed of the King that is all, what I want to
know is this why should all men suffer and wives and
children be parted from one another and not only that
being killed at the same time just to suit the King's greed
that is all and I cannot see the use of it at all can you
dear, I did not tell you Mrs Bigham has got Tommy to
mind for me dear and you see it is not very far when I
come home to go for him and he is much happier there
than round the other place dear well dear I cant see
ending to this rotten war I am proply [properly]
heartsick of it all and if it was not for thinking of you so
much I should have to give way and by your letter dear
you seem to think just as I do never mind we must make
the best of it dear there is no other way out of it dear
never mind always think of me of as your sweet little
wife and sweetheart Lizzie little Tommy sends his best
love and lots of kisses and is keeping your place warm in
bed for you dear.

74 Ossory Road
Old Kent Rd

April 24th [1918]

Dear Tom
Just a line in answer to your welcome letter which I
received this morning dear. I am pleased you are keeping
well dear and still going great I am glad you have
received an instructor's certificate, I suppose you past
out top. I am not feeling very grand myself the weather
is very trying, rain rain rain day after day it get on your
nerves and the raids are giving me a teasing I can tell you
although we have come off alright up till now dear thank
goodness, all the large buildings and churches and
schools have all got sandbags piled up but never mind
Gods good and he is the only one to look to for help and
he has took care of us and we must trust in him dear,
with regards to the war it seem just as bad as ever no
ending at all never mind live in hope that is all. I quite
understand the sun dear I thought you were 5 hours
later than we were, Jack is better and is in France again
don't give them much time in England dear I can tell
you it must be terrible in France now properly murder
there. I must tell you Kate is engaged to Harry seems he
has been home from France wounded and he has been
sent back again a week ago, stone Ginger with them both
Thumbs up. With regards to Tommy he is a tinker up to
every thing talks to Mrs Bragg like an old man he is a
happy little chap and when the raids are on he is not at
all nervous takes it very cool when the guns are so loud
he says my earholes you Germans but more often than
not he goes off to sleep, he plays take cover and all clear.

Hear [here] I close hoping to find you in the best of health I remain your loving wife Lizzie

74 Ossory Rd
Old Kent Rd

April 25th [1918]

Dearest
Just a line in answer to another letter I am sorry you lost
your stripe but it just as well dear don't you think so I
am pleased to hear the heat does not affect you dear, I
have got the ring safe and sound dear and I am very
pleased with it I think it is beautiful dear and very
uncommon I also received the locket and chain I like it
very much it is very kind of you to think of me so much,
by your letter you are keeping very well and I am pleased
to hear you say you are as strong as a horse and as lively
as a cricket, don't get to[o] lively out [or] you will have
to put it out the window old boy. I suppose you are
keeping alright down there your son is getting a nut I
have just smack[ed] his hand for doing something
annoying me he did cry, got under the table to look for
something to hit me back and what do you thi[nk] he
got a ginger beer bottle, and made this remark to hiself I
wont half give her a wap [whack]. I cant help laughing
the weather is very miserable raining three parts of the
time had a letter from the Post-Office with regard to
parcel saying they was not responable [responsible] for
breakage dear so I don't [k]now what can be done dear
there was the bracelet and the little box that got broke
dear hear [here] I close hoping this will not be long
before you are home has [as] I am breaking my heart for
you dear you [k]now it is such a hunger feeling nothing
see[m] to feel dear and at time it seem to get on you
worse dear if only you were coming home tomorrow
dear I feel I should go mad it['s] a rotten life dear make
no mistake about it shawley [surely] there must be an

ending I should not care so long as I was hear [here]
with you dear that is all I [k]now hear [here] I close
hoping you are in the best of health Lizzie

74 Ossory Rd
Old Kent Rd

May 1 [1918]

Dearest
Just a line hoping you are quite well as it leaves us both
at present, Well dear I do hope this war will soon be
over, as I am nearly breaking my heart to see you dear

I did not think it would come so hard as it has parting
with you, although I know I should miss you very much
dear but I don't know what it is but I sometimes wonder
if I shall see you dear which I hope and trust I do as
sometimes it seem to turn my head when I think of you
being away three years as people tell me you will be dear
to get propley climitex [properly acclimatised] to India do
you think there is any truth in it dear, sometimes I think I
shall not live another day without you dear Oh it is such a
rotten life, you couldn't hardly image [imagine] what it is
like dear, never mind you cannot help it I [k]now, when
you do come home I will never lose you I can tell you it
make you get dresprite [desperate] I can tell you, the King
and Queen don't suffer only the likes of us and it does not
come so hard to some people as they do not love as we do
dear sometime I wish I did not love so much, then it
would[n't] hurt so much it [is] a sort of pain and I cannot
get rid of it dear I expect it serves you just the same dear
never mind there must be an end to all things and it must
come to an end, but the worse of it is you cannot seem to
see the end of it dear and I suppose we must keep on
smiling dear and when you do come I shall hang on you
for dear life I can tell you dear Hear [here] I close hoping
it will not be long before I see you dear I remain

Your loving wife Lizzie

74 Ossory Rd
Old Kent Rd

May 5th [1918]

Dearest
Just a line hoping you are quite well as it leaves us both
at present, Well dear everything is going on alright at
home and there is no need for you to worry about us
dear. Little Tommy is well and is as cheeky as anything
he will soon be four years old, the end of this month he
is such a fine boy getting quite big and nice looking and
he can't help eat just like a young horse, he says he is
going to school when he is 5 if anyone ask him. Well
dear I have got some news for you dear, your brother
Bob is going to get married Whitsun to that girl of his,
your father don't say much, but at the same time he does
not like it, but what will be will be and it does not do to
have anythink to say, your Carrie is getting along alright
quite her old self dear, I do hope this war is over soon
dear and you will come home to us alright, it seem a
shame for people to have to suffer like this dear you
know it seem the same of things over and over again, it
must be rotten for you dear so far away and no chance
never mind so long as we keep well dear I think that is
something to be thankful for dear well dear hear [here] I
close hoping to find you well as it leaves us both at
present I remain your loving wife Lizzie

PS I received your letter asking for socks etc I have had
to order them dear as they are very scarce and I expect I
shall be sending them in a few days dear Just think dear
this is Sunday night 8/o/c I am writing this letter some
of the misable [miserable] Sunday evenings I have ever
had dear through no fault of our own never mind
cheerio till we meet

74 Ossory Rd
Old Kent Rd

May 9th [1918]

Dear Daddy
I got the postal order alright for which I thank you very
much I have told mama to take me to the post office and
I have got a bank book all for myself. I hope you are
happy and I do wish you were coming home as mama
and I miss you very much. I shall save up a lot as I get a
lot of pennies given me. Daddy dear I cannot write
myself so I got mama to answer this letter and if you
send me a lot of letters I know she will write to you for
me, and when I go to school and learn I will then write
to you daddy. I am a good boy to my mam and I am
taking great care of her so you need not worry over her
at all, I like my present very much and I thin[k] you are
a good daddy to send them to me I will take great care of
them and have them when you come home which I hope
will not be long hear [here] I close thanking you again
and again for my birthday presents and hoping to see
you soon

I am your loving son

Tommy

74 Ossory Rd
Old Kent Rd

May 10th [1918]

Dearie
Just a line in answer to your letter which I received safe
and sound and the 3 pounds as well which I thank you
very much dear it is very kind of you to send it dear you
must think of us a lot dear, as I think of you always in
my thoughts and mind dear and life get quite miserable
at times dear I can tell you never mind it must be rotten
life for you too but there must be an ended some day
and the sooner the better what say, you ask how much is
in the bank dear £50-17-10 that is the exact amount dear
I should have like it more but when you have to give 1/6
for a tin of milk and 2/8lb tea and no meat under 1/8lb
that is only pieces dear you can guess how things are
never mind we keep on smiling that is the only thing to
do I cannot buy a pair of shoes under 18/6 and little
Tommy the very cheapest is 6/11 so you can see dear.
You ask about Tommy little sister well by the time you
come home I shall be a maid and we shall have to start
afresh I shall not mind so long as you don't want me to
find the hole and another thing don't wrisetl [wrestle]
with me like you did first go off, I expect it got out of
control at time the only thing is to give it a wack and
keep it quiet for a time dear so take great care of it and
fetch it home safe and sound and good looking and bare
[bear] in mind what I am saying. You ask after Squibb he
is getting on alright like married life alright, nothing
better had she known she would have got married before
but kiddies are out of the question and another thing
she is quite disgusted if you ask her about little Maudie
or Bert I can tell you. I expect it must have been hard at

first when you had to go without your bit of culture
never mind these things will happen, as regards to Kate
and Grace I think they have forgotten where we live as
regards the old Girl I am done with her as I find it best
dear hear [here] I close hoping you will like this letter
and post your remarks about it in the next one dear
from your loving and longing wife Lizzie

Turn over –
I received parcel and locket and ring but the box in the
parcel was broken and the Braclet [bracelet] dear hard
luck don't you think so.

74 Ossory Rd
Old Kent Rd
May 23rd [1918]

Dearest
Just a line hoping to find you in the pink of health as it
leaves us at present, Well dear I am feeling much better
than I did at the beginning of the week as we had a big
air raid and they make [me] fell [feel] low of course you
know Jack is in France again has been out there 3 month
again in your letter dear you say it is your greatest desire
to be back with us dear I feel as hungry as anything just
to be with you dear and now I have got you for good
dear nothing on earth seem to comfort me dear
sometimes it seem harder to bear, I think how we love
one another it is the most sinful thing on earth to part
us as we are parted and make our heart long and yearn,
some people do not know what it is to love and of
course it make no difference to them, but when it comes
to parting two lovers as we are, it's a real sin don't you
think so dear, my letter may sound selfish but I cannot
help it dear I do love you so, and you know it is true love
dear and no spruce about it, I often feel I have not been
as I should be to you but it has been for our own good as
I have only got the one child to look after when if we had
been silly there might have been 3 or 4 children instead
Tommy is off hand now and I can earn a shilling where I
should have been hampered with more, never mind
when you come home I will make it up to you dear, I
won't care about what becomes of me then dear, here
[here] I close hoping you are quite well I remain your
loving wife

74 Ossory Rd
Old Kent Rd

May 26th [?1918]

[incomplete]

Dearest
Just a line in answer to your welcome letter which I
received yesterday I am glad you are quite well dear it is
just a week ago that we had a very bad air raid dear and
they dropped bombs at the top of the street but I am
feeling more of myself today I have just come out of the
bath I know you would like to have been at home to
have seen me, little Tommy is getting very noisy I can tell
you I have wash[ed] my head you [k]now one of those
nice washes I used to have I felt quite bright for it I can
tell you dear I was glad you got my letters as it is rotten
waiting like you have and not hearing from home, with
regards to buying me something dear you must not keep
spending your money on me but if you come across a
nice bracelet I should like that very much dear but don't
put yourself out dear as I have got that ring it is beautiful
I ware [wear] it on my second finger as it is a bit to[o]
big and slip off the three finger, in your letter dear I
notice you spoke of our children I hope you wont go in
for stock when you come home as I am not made for a
lot of kiddies you ask after Miss Brooks she has left Mr
Savage has gone to Bucks for during the war out of raids
her husband is a discharge soldier and his nerves are bad
he think it is best so I have not seen her for a month
these raids are playing up hell with the people hear
[here], I can tell you, I am not as brave as I used to be
but never mind we must trust to God help and he will
look after us dear, as regards to George address I have
sent it to you and you should have...

74 Ossory Rd
Old Kent Rd

[June] [1918]

Dearest
Just a line in answer to your letter which I received on
June 6th well dear am sorry to hear that you are
attending hospital I hope and trust it is not serious, well
dear we are both keeping very well, your carrie has had a
offer to take a house at brighton already furnished and
let it for somebody and she wants me to go with her to
helping the work of the house. I been thinking about it
dear but have not decided on it what do you think about
it dear. We have had our photo taken and I am sending it
on dear I have not come out as nice as I should dear
never mind I shall have some more done and then I shall
let you have them dear. When are you going to send me
one of your photos as you promised. You know that
chap Fred that lived in Auley Street well he has been
killed on 27th May so we must think ourselves lucky up
to now well dear I hope you are alright as it must be very
trying out there for you. Old Arthur is going on alright
dear up to now Hear [here] I close hoping you are going
alright I remain your loving wife

Lizzie

74 Ossory Rd
Old Kent Road

June 25th [1918]

Dearie

Just a line in answer to your most welcome letter I
received, Well dear I am very pleased to hear that you are
B III as that will stop you being sent to the firing line
dear I am very pleased about it but should be more so if
I [k]new you was sent home dear but never mind we
must be thankful for what we have had dear. Well dear I
have received the £3 alright and I think you will be
pleased to know that we have got £57-7-10 in the bank
up till writing his letter not so bad is it but I could have
done better never mind I tried to save more but things
are so dear that I couldn't, now dear you as[k] Carrie's
address it is 130 South Street but she has gone away to
Worthing until the war is over out of the air raids, we
have been having a rough time but things have been
quite [quiet] this last 3 weeks thank goodness and we
can do with it to[o], Young Tommy is a brick he take no
notice of the raids, and he plays take cover, called
Goodbyee and the kiddies sing a dittie to it and Tommy
know it he sing all day long, this is it goodbye don't cryee
5-20 Gotha in the skyee when the maroon go off, should
a bomb drop near, we is Goodbyee, with regards to the
scarves dear I gave Carrie the cream one to her as she
has been very kind to me and I don't forget any people
that are good to us dear, Well I am sorry to say I cannot
get on with Flo, and I have tried to I can tell you, she
seem always trying to cut you up, if you can make out
what I mean, now with regards to money matters she
keeps on about what she has save up she forgets she had
about 12 months start and then on top of that the

dividend from Hartleys every time it come round, she is
so selfish, she even quarill [quarrelled] with Carrie who
has been a good friend to her as you [k]now, she has got
that feeling that everybody is beholding to her and I
have got nothing to be grateful to her for and if she
wants to be funny with me she will have to get on with it
that['s] all as she is not the only one that has got there
husband away but she think so I can tell you never mind
we wont talk about her as it is not very fetching I can tell
you she is mean. The Post Office have wrote and told me
that they do not stand responsible for breakages so I
shall let the matter drop that is all, Well dear with
regards to six or eight kiddies I don't think it matters I
should very much like to have a little girl and Tommy
would be off hand so I think it would be very nice dear
and as you [k]now I always did like girls, but it is rather
a funny thing to write about dear but I am quite cold
minded about it and I really mean it I daresay you will
smile when you read this, but it just what I have got in
my mind dear, I said when you was home I should not
like any more, but that was because I used to think of the
time I had, now I feel much stronger I should not mind,
never mind if go on talking like this I shall make you
think you are at home and your mouth might water, but
don't forget it must be a girl or I shall cancel the
contract. I must close dear I remain your loving wife
Lizzie and love from little Tommy.

74 Ossory Road
Old Kent Road

June 28th [1918]

Dearest just a line in answer to your welcome letter
dated 15/5/18 Well dear I am pleased to hear you are
going alright With regards to your falling in love at first
sight dear what made you do it write and tell me dear,
You ask after Mr Ward Well he has had to join he has
been away 3 months know [now] and has not been
home yet he was [has] been made a clerk w[h]ere he was
station, Well dear I am sorry to say Freddy Ward that
was with you at Wiltshire has been killed on the 24th
May and Harry Evans Kates young man has been
missing since the 27th May of course you [k]now they
were engaged don't you and Kate is upset about it to[o],
I will write and let you [k]now if I get any news about
him dear, with regards to George and Jack I don't seem
to get in touch with anyone that knows about them. Well
dear in your letters you seem to have a lot to say about
our children I hope you are not looking forward to a lot
as that would never do, has [as] I say I do not mind
going in for another one but no more, so keep that in
mind. With regards to you being past Blll I am very
pleased indeed anything sooner than you being sent to
France or where the murdering is going on as you
cannot call it anything else dear it so alful [awful] for
words don't you think so, with regards to taxes and the
price of food and clothes and boots it make one sick to
go shoping [shopping] now I know you would not like
to go shoping [shopping] with me as it saves a meal for
when you get home you are fed up with the prices and
you don't want anything to eat I can tell you dear, never
mind it wont last for ever, there one thing you can get a

little and make sure of it with these coupons that we
have now you get some, and that is more than we used
to be able to do, we have meat tickets and tea sugar and
margarine cards and each week we have it book[ed] so
you can only get one lot and no more but still that is
better than waiting in queues and having sometimes
nothing as I have often waited perhaps ½ hour or 1 hour
and then sold out, You seem to get things very cheap out
there it is a pleasure to hear somethings are going cheap
even if you cannot get near to buy, I am very
comfortable though at times I get very lonely but little
Tommy is a great comfort to me dear, and I can quite
understand people that have got their husbands away
and have got a lot of children they seem very happy dear
with there [their] little ones it takes the loneliness off a
lot dear I was very pleased with that ring dear and it
look very smart dear and if you can get a lot of those
brass things I should like them very much but don't send
anything home that is going to break as coming such a
long way the post people wont be responsible for it dear,
Well dear I must close with Kind love and Kisses I
remain your loving wife

Lizzie
xxxxxxxx These are from little Tommy
xxxxxxxx and these are for you dear

74 Ossory Road
Old Kent Rd

[undated – from context July 1918]

Dearest
Just a line hoping to find you in the pink of health as it
leaves me at present, Well Dear it is nearing our wedding
day dear 5 years it don't seem to be so long as that, I have
nothing to regret only that I have lost two years and 3
months through being parted from you dear which I feel
at time that it is more than I can put up with, I know it is
quite as misable [miserable] for you if not more so dear,
I often picture you as you used to be at home when we
used to go out together, dear, only those that are placed
as we are and are all in all to one another, they are the
ones that relizes [realise] what it is, but those who have
led a cat and dog life are the ones that don't care dear
there is a young woman that live next door, her husband
is in Egypt they were very happy together dear until the
war parted them, as it has us, and then it few and far
between that understand your feelings dear, it is very
hard to make people understand your loss all you get in
return, is "Well you ought to think yourself lucky that he
is alive["] not a kind word from anyone, just because
they are lucky enough to have there husband at home
with them this is a poor world for finding comfort and
so called friend dear and I expect you are placed the
same, but never mind dear it cannot last for ever and
then we shall meet again dear, hoping never to part, for
this has taught us a lesson dear and I think we quite
understand the loss of one another dear, I hope you are
not worrying about us we are quite alright but as I say it
is a rotten life for us both and the longer you are away
the worse it gets dear as I expect you find it the same,

Well dear I thought of going away for a week holiday
down to Worthing that is where your sister Carries is
dear and it will do us good as I have been very much run
down dear, as the price of food and boots and clothing is
most alful [awful] dear it is all a trouble dear, never
mind I think I shall be able to manage a week dear, I
only wish you was at home to go with us it would be fine
dear don't you think so if this war was to finish soon do
you think you would come home or would you have to
stop out there for 3 years after dear, as someone told me
you would, I cant belived [believe] that dear, I hope you
don't think I am upset dear but you [k]now what it is, it
[? eases] the mind to speak out and when it come round
to 5 years dear it make you think a bit, as regard to your
son he does get big and quite a man in his way I can tell
you things he says to me you would hardly belived
[believe] it, it's a wonder how he remember it, he is right
off hand now and I am sure you would be pleased to see
him, even when I come home tired dear he help to take
my boots off gets the cups off the dresser go for the milk
off the milkman and ever so many things he run for, and
can open the street door without a chair, you [k]now it
is nearly 12 month since you see him dear he has
alter[ed] a lot from a baby to a big boy I can tell you you
will have to behave yourself when you come home has
[as] you wont stand a chance, he fight the boys in the
street no one can have it on with him dear, and it['s] just
as well, as I have to leave him like I do

Well dear I think this is all at present

I remain your most loving wife Lizzie

74 Ossory Rd
Old Kent Rd

July 3rd [1918]

Dearest
Just a line hoping you are quite well as it leaves us at
present. Well dear we have got ak[n] illness which is
called the Spanish Flue and it is raging most awful dear
there are people dying with it. The man has come home
from work with it you have to take to your bed with it
they say it takes all the use of your limbs away and
people are dropping down with it dear isn't it awful I do
hope you are well and comfortable dear I say I shall
make you smile when I tell you I have got £60 in the
bank dear I know you will be pleased about it and 6
shillings for Tommy dear that is grand isn't it that's the
stuff to give em I can tell you dear my work has been
very plentiful just lately dear and it makes it all the better
for me I have got my book close on £14 per week so that
makes my com [?commission] more and the order have
gone very nicely so I have been doing well dear I thought
I would tell you as I know it will please you well dear do
you think you will be sent home there are a lot of people
who I have spoke to about you said that you will dear I
hope there is some truth behind it dear I suppose I told
you that Shannons have moved they have got a house at
the top of the street dear those that got up the steps and
the people who have got the house now are very nice
they are both soldiers wives and one has had her
husband away 3 years and he is in Egypt and the other's
husband is expecting to go to France anyday but they are
very nice I can tell you they have little Tommy for me
while I go to work as that person upstairs as [has] had to
turn out to work, I gave him to Mrs Bygman she had

him for a while and then got tired of him as soon as
Georgie went to school, she can afford to hold her head
up her old man has got another 6 months exemption
another one let me down on a Saturday dear I found
someone and he is very happy in there they have got a
little girl only 2 years old and father is in Egypt and has
never seen her she is a sweet little kid and young Tommy
loves her they get on well together I can tell you her
name is Millie and all I can hear about is his little Mill as
soon as I come home they are as happy as sandboys
together I can tell you dear, you [know] what it is they
want the money and not the trouble of the child, I still
pay the same money for him dear and give a ¼ of butter
every week and them 3 slices of jam for luck so I think I
pay alright don't you, I don't want to give up my work if
I can help it dear as it is a light job and I get a few days a
week off and it suit me very well of course it is hard
while I am at it dear of course he is a very loving child
and that is why people like him dear, Well dear I must
close has [as] I am getting very tried [tired] and it is late
dear I am going to bed I always think of you at night and
I often wake up from dreaming of you dear you was
always very kind to me dear that is why I close with
fondest love and kisses I remain your loving wife Lizzie

74 Ossory Road
Old Kent Rd

July 9th [1918]

Dear Tom
Just a line hoping you are quite well, I have been very
queer with the Spanish Flue very bad indeed light
headed so they told me, I have been home for a week
dear I wrote to Savage and he did not answer nore [nor]
send anybody down whether he is frightened of catching
it or weather [whether] it is because he is wild I don't
[k]now but there it is, if feeling alright Saturday I shall
make a start again I hope but I am going on alright now
dear so don't worry about me as I am quite comfortable
and I expect my work is alright when I am ready to start
again, you know dear this new complaint is very ?
[catching] there are over 1000 in the arsnel [? Arsenal]
with it and no end of shops have closed down for a time,
little Tommy is alright up till now and I do hope he
keeps so, this war is very trying and one don't seem so
strong as they used to be dear, and I expect that is what
it is, never mind I have written to Carrie asking her to
try and put us up for a week dear August that might do
us good which I think the change will do so I hope it
will, Well dear I want to speak to you about the bank
with regards to anything happening to you or myself it is
very funny to think about but I should [k]now what to
do in such a case I want you to let me know just who
[how] it stand dear if anything should happen so just let
me know wont you dear

Hear [here] I close hoping to find you in the pink of health

I remain your loving wife
Lizzie

74 Ossory Road
Old Kent Rd

July 9th

[1918-? wrong date in month – after she has had Spanish flu]
[incomplete]

Dearie
Just a line in answer to your letter which I received this
morning with 2 others quite unexpected, I was so taken
back dear for I had two letters from the last mail which
was in 3 weeks ago, you say there is no ending to this
war, well I cant see it ever coming to an end from the
very first as I used to say to you dear when you were at
home dear Well dear I am sorry my spelling is so rotten
as you say you must speak to your son about it just you
think nine time out of ten he is up to his trick but while
I am writing this letter he happen to be engaged in
something in the garden and I can think out what I want
to put in the letter dear that is if he stop there, Well dear
he is in everything and up to everything I can tell you,
and at time I lose my temper with him, he is above a
joke I can tell you but never mind take him all round he
not so bad I am sorry if you cannot understand my
letters but you forget times have altered and we are
learning French that is a little of it I have been sending
you just lately Well dear they have sent George to Egypt I
have not got his address yet but when I do I will let you
[k]now, by your letters you are having a lively time but
hotter than it should be for comfort dear I am sorry that
you are not so comfortable as I thought but as people
have got the idea in there head that you are it is no doing
of mine I can tell you most of your people reckon you
are very lucky and I ought to be pleased at you being

there but I myself cannot see it perhaps I want glasses I
don't [k]now if that['s] it, in my last letter I told you I
had been very queer with the Spanish Flue well I going
on very nicely now and feeling myself again so don't...

74 Ossory Rd
Old Kent Rd

July 15 [1918]

Dearie
Just a line hoping to find you in the pink of health as it
leaves us both at present Well dear I must say I am
feeling much better, I have been very queer but am going
great now, I am going to have a week's holiday August
down at Worthing dear with Carrie she is going to have
us and charge me 12/6 for a week which I think is very
cheap and it will do us good to[o] as the boy is run
down and a week at the seaside will do us the world of
good just picture young Tommy picking up shells from
the sands dear, I know you would like to be with us and
shouldn't I like you there to[o] it would be the happiest
time of my life but never mind God good and he will
spare us a time together if it his will, which I hope it is
dear, such a longing come over me at time dear for to
have you as I used to sometimes I cannot contain myself,
then I think God as [has] been good to us and spared us
for one another up till now dear it is a most trying time
for both of us to be parted and to [k]now that we love
each other as we do, but it is better to [k]now that we
can trust each other and that feeling consoles us don't it
dear. Well dear you might think I am rather silly to write
as I do but if I write you a letter like this I feel I am
talking to you dear I can often picture you in the
armchair with your paper and when I used to come and
sit on your lap how you would throw it down and then
cuddle me how I miss all those little ways, this life make
one feel tired as we are missing great things which were
made for us, to keep us bright dear but never mind be
greatful [grateful] we are spared and may yet continued

to be so until we are reunited again which I hope will
not be long now dear, Well dear I have had a man down
from Rye Lane about the teeth they was very saucy and I
told them off they got more than they wanted one came
yesterday and the other today I don't know what they are
going to do I think they [k]now it is a hot customer to
dill [deal] with don't blame me do you dear trying to
bank me to pay the balance and then have another lot
made, but I was not having any, I tick them off I can tell
you dear, leave it to me I have not been on my own for 2
years for nothing I told them when they caught me
napping once but not again, I will let you know how it
goes off dear Well dear I have been doing the front room
up and it do look pretty dear I was just thinking how
you would like to peep in the door I [k]now you would
like to see it, it look a picture dear I can tell you so lovely
the chairs keep as good as ever dear, it would cost
something to buy that lot now dear I can tell you for
things are an alful [awful] price now, I priced a wardrobe
and they ask me £15 for it and a sideboard £20 so you
can bet money would not buy our little home now
which is very pretty when everything is in place dear,
Well dearie I must close as Tommy is going to sleep on
the table I remain still

Your loving wife Lizzie

74 Ossory Rd
Old Kent Rd

July 26th [1918]

Dearest
Just a line hoping to find you in the best of health as it
leaves us both at present Well dear we are h[av]ing very
bad weather for the time of year dear storms and rain in
buckets full dear Well dear you will be surprised to know
George is in Egypt there is not much to say dear is a
puzzle to know what to put in the letters dear I am
sitting hear [here] thinking to myself what to put and I
expect you are the same when you write to me dear
We[ll] dear to begin with I wish this rotten war was over
then we should not have to write to each other, buy [by]
the way dear Harry Evans is reported missing which
sound very ? [ominous] the red Cross report him
missing this is 9 weeks it is very sad dear don't you think
so, We must think ourself lucky dear as God has been
very good to us and spare us and safe guarded us up to
now dear and we must trust him to look after us in the
future dear it is a most alful [awful] time before every
body dear, sad and misable [miserable] dear, and at
times as much as one can put up with, but then that
feeling come into you that you are very lucky to be spare
up to now it is a comfort dear, I am very silly to write to
you in this fashion but I do love you so and so
pass[ion]ate that it is as much as I can keep myself
together dear I do love you when I was single I used to
spar with chaps but speaking the truth I don't think I
ever loved of them, even that Dick Martin was very nice
in his way but I cant say I like him any more than
friendly he has been in London for his training dear
from New Zealand, went and see them at home was

quite surprise[d] to [k]no[w] to[o] I was married so
Kate said, he has gone to France dear Kate said he has
not altered a bit still his old way he is not married I
soppose [suppose] no one will have him dear, if he could
only [k]now that I was so happy as I was with you dear
but I don't think anyone would understand dear as we
were out of the usual with one another dear, kind good
hearted and thoughtful dear and that is why we got on
dear together as we do dear, and in return we had a nice
little son one anyone could be proud of I can tell you
dear, if he goes on as he do he will be a credit to us, I
hope the army don't claim him when he is old enough
dear as that is what I have been hearing when they are
old enough dear but that is a long time to look forward
to dear yet, and I hope we shall live in better times then
dear, Jack is alright up till the 21st of this month dear I
am pleased he is keeping well because of the children
dear I expect you find it very lonely out there dear and
miss us very much dear as we do you and making no
friends it make it very hard for anyone dear but never
mind it cant last for ever dear and that is why we stand
up as we do Well dear I must close hoping you are in the
pink of health as it leaves me and Tommy at present I
remain your loving wife Lizzie

Kisses sent from Tommyxxxxxxxxxxxxxxxxx
And these are from your old cuddlie
xxxxxxxxxxxxxxxxxxx

74 Ossory Rd
Old Kent Rd

Aug 18th [1918]

Dearie
Just a line hoping you are quite well dear as it leaves us
both at present little Tommy is getting a bonny kid and
is growing so big, I am shur [sure] you would be
surprised if you could just see him dear I think such a lot
of him and he does of me I can tell you, he get quite
concerned over me if I am not well, he keep coming to
me and saying, are you getting better Mum, he is the best
of kids I can tell you, Well dear me and Carrie [h]as had
a falling out not had a row but there is a difference
between us all over young Tommy and those two kids of
hers of course you know I went to Worthing for a week,
well before that Carrie went down there and where she is
staying the woman has gone to Leeds to her husband, so
Carrie takes over the house for this said woman, takes
the visitors on just as if the woman was doing it herself, I
write to Carrie asking her if she could let us come down
and I would pay her as if I was the same as a visitor for
the week, she writes back and said come by all means, I
am kid[d]ing myself I would have a good week's rest and
change when I get down there she has got the cheek to
come up to London and stop a couple of days, and on
top of that she leaves me to see to her visitors and also
her two kids which are both buggers and on top of that
lot expect me to pay the 12/6 for the week and no bed to
lay on for me and the boy, I feel happy you may be shur
[sure], while [? Arthie] paid [?laid] into my Tommy like
a navvy and cheek me as well the snotty nose [?worm],
when I told her I cannot see where I ow[e] her the 12/6
as I had not got a bed to sleep on no[r] a room to put

my clothes in, she said I wanted to be funny, she herself
had to sleep in the kitchen on a chiar [chair] bedstead
which a woman across the road lent her, she knew when
she told me to come down that she had no place to put
us and my boy wants his rest as well as others dear, the
first night I sleep with her that made 5 of us on the
single chair bedstead but you can guess how much sleep
I had with two great big kids kicking like they do at
night, and it was kind of the other visitors that let me
share her bed with her or that would have had to last a
week, and what made me worse wild she had that man
who had your book, insurance you know name of Boyce
and his wife and kiddee down there and she is telling the
other visitors that I am coming down to see to them
while she comes up to London, making me quite cheap
to them and at the same time taking 3 weeks money
where she ought to only have two and forgetting that I
could see what her game was, when I get down there she
comes up to London and left me do the dirty work and
on top of that expect me to pay for the bed I never had
but not this child I can tell you I have been caught but I
am much wiser now dear she has wrote to her Bill and
pitch up a very good tale to him, as when I went round
for the pair of stay[s] I left there he said don't come here
any more I am surprise at you, I said you shouln't
[shouldn't] get surprise at any thing until you know the
facts of the case, he said don't come her[e] anymore, I
said, right, Carrie said that Bill was doing bad and she
must make so[me] money this end, meaning Worthing,
I said yes that is all very well, but get it honest not rob
and bleed people which I think is nothing else, she is
better but she is a proper mean thing I myself am
surprise at her trying to put it on me like that she knew I
have saved some money and that was what she thought
she would get 12'6 on the quick but it was I who caught

her, another thing that Mr Boyce has got running sor[e]s
on his legs and she said to me before she went up to
London when the insurance people goes you and Jinnie
and Arthie can go in that bed, so I change the sheets
before we went to bed, and she didn't half rap off
because they was for some more visitors that was coming
I told her never mind about the visitors I don't want
sor[e]s all over me but she didn't like it I can tell you
dear but I don't care those that laugh last always laugh
hearty and my turn is coming dear I expect, well dear no
doubt you will be cross at me over this af[f]air but it had
to be I cannot have people come in to[o] much I think
myself that Carrie had a cheek to get me down there to
suit her own self and that is all it amount to, but write
and tell me what you think about it there was just 21
people in that house and not so big as ours dear there
was only 5 rooms and washhouse in all so you can just
see how it was dear I am sorry it happened but it cant be
helped dear hoping you will not think no less of me for it

Hear [here] I close hoping you are keeping quite well I
remain your loving wife Lizzie

PS I have not received that £7 yet that is a week ago
when you said it was coming by that post and I got ten
letters

PS She told the visitors that I was coming down to see to
them but not a word to me about it until she was going
up to London not so bad me go to get the sea air and
have to be the servant for the visitors She did not care
about me losing money this end to have a week rest oh
no that was nothing and that is just what it was I left my
round because I wanted the change and that is how she
served me dear

74 Ossory Road
Old Kent Road

[undated] [from context August 1918]

Dearest,
Just a line to let you know we are in the best of health as
I hope you are dear Well dear I have had a week holiday
with Carrie at Worthing dear and not enjoyed myself a
bit I am surprised at Carrie treating me as she has dear. I
wrote and asked her if she could have me for a week and
of course pay for my bedroom dear, made all the
arrangements 7 weeks ago, left my work for the week
expecting to have a good holiday dear. I go down there
and find she has filled the room with other visitors so I
had to sleep on a bedstead with her, only 5 of us in it is a
bit thick and of course she expected me to pay 12/6 for
the bedroom that I never had. I keep myself and instead
of getting out a bit I had to stop in and get ready for the
other people that she has got stopping there. And on top
of that she wants me to pay the 12/6 so I had a couple of
words about it. You don't blame me do you, young
Archie was for everlasting fighting young Tommy and
Jennie as well dear. I was glad to get home dear. It cost
me 17/- for fares and all the five days I was there I only
got out once to see the sea. She even came up to London
and stopped for 2 days and left me to see to the visitors
there. Don't you think she had a cheek and do the
housework as well. Left those two kids and they played
me up alright I can tell you, kicked young Tommy awful
and when she asked them if they did they said no and
she never believed me at all. I was disgusted at her I can
tell you, should Jennie write to you don't send her any
presents as they paid little Tommy awful. They thought I
should let it pass off but I am not so silly as I used to be

and I am not going to let people put on him as he is only a baby and I noticed that when you haven't got a man behind you people try and take liberties, but it is not coming off here. I had to put my foot down with my own people and I am afraid I shall have to step in with yours dear, as I cannot understand this blood-sucking business and Carrie is not going to try it on me. I don't want you to make any trouble — let her think I have not said anything to you about it, and don't forget don't send them children anything as they are not worth it dear. I am sorry I have had to write to you like this but I don't think it is fair for children to be made a fuss of when Carrie is so rotten to try and put it on me dear, no doubt you will wonder what is the matter with me dear. I am alright only I like people to be fair, dear. Times are hard enough without your own people trying to crush you dear. If you think I have done wrong let me know but I don't think so. Well dear I am pleased to get all these letters from you. Fancy, 10 by 2 post dear and then you ought to get quite a lot dear — this is the first dear which I hope you won't think very nasty dear.

Hear [here] I close

Hoping you are well

I remain yours
Lizzie

74 Ossory Rd
Old Kent Rd
London
SE1

Aug 19 [1918]

Dearie

Just a line in answer to your most welcome letters which
I received all together dear, I am pleased you are getting
along nicely dear as we are to be expected to be the same
dear under the surcs [circs] Well dear I expect you have
received that letter by now telling you of our weeks
holiday dear I am sorry I had to tell Carrie my mind but
it was her own fault, and perhaps it is just as well, so as
to let her see she cannot do it on me. Well dear it nearly
time we spoke of ourselves dear I am glad you think I
am managing things at home well for as you relies
[realise] times are very bad hear [here], and of course
boots and clothes are a price I can tell you dear fancy
10/- for a pair of shoes and 12/6 for boots little Tommy
he takes a 8 in size now dear you ask me if I can ware
[wear] boots now, well I can and I should like you to see
what I have got on dear they come right up my leg and
look very smart to[o] And I am shur [sure] you would
be pleased if you saw them dear they cost 35/6 and cheap
at that as this very day you cannot buy the same boot for
that money dear, as for costumes I have not trouble
about as I cannot get one to suit my taste under £5 so I
am hanging on my blue one still and it look just as good
as ever, you ask me how the Front Room look it is just
the same as ever dear rich and bright, with regards to the
piano I was going to ask you about it there is only £1-5
to pay and don't you think they ought to tune it before it
is paid up for dear just you write and let me know what

you think of it dear as I think they ought , Well dear I
have got some bad news to tell you I am sorry to say that
our Charlie wife nell has died she was bury last
Thursday dear, she was 3month ½ and she went to the
Southwark Pk Rd on Friday and got knock down with a
motor car it shuck [shook] her up as they though[t] and
she was put to bed, Well they sent for a doctor and he
order her to a hospital, they could not have operation
owning to the heart being week so of course poison set
up in the inside and killed her it is awful thing don't you
think so dear little Nellie is staying with her auntie on
nell side and the child do not know her mother is dead
yet she is 5 years old sad isnt it dear just you think it
might have been me when Tommy was a fortnight old
dear, as it something of that kind I was suffering from,
but God was good to me and took care of me so I should
look after Tommy while you were away dear, Well dear
let us talk of something cheering how it is still as good as
ever take great care of it as I shall over-hall [overhaul] it
when you come home don't forget to make it smart and
presentable with regards to myself it would surprise you
it is better looking than ever that makes you wild I bet,
never mind I am sorry you cant have your own back
owning to the long distance away, but live in hope for
better time dear what do you think of it,

Well dear this is all I have to say at present

I remain your loving wife

[Fragment. August 1918 – the dispute with Carrie – see other letters]

...least, with regards to the whole fortnight I think I can account for that dear I was in bed very ill with the flue it has been in London a raer [rare] lot and people have been dying with it dear but thank God I got on very well I went Worthing to Carrie for a week after I got up thinking it would do me good and then fell in for all the work while she come up to London for a couple of days, left her two kids for me to look after and me feeling so queer and all, you bet I felt happy to[o] and all, the visitors that were staying there I had to see to them, well I can tell you I was surprise[d] at her and what is more throughly [thoroughly] disgusted with it all I suppose your people will look down on me because I spoke my mind but I don't care in the least I shall not go and see any of them, you can please yourself...

4 Ossory Road
Old Kent Rd.
SE1
London

Aug 20 [1918]
(2)

Dearest
Just a line hoping you are quite well as it leaves us both
at present Well dear with regards to numbering the
letters I think is a very good idea, with regards to Jack, he
his [is] in France dear been out since April I think he is
keeping well up till now dear old Bill Pascoe has got
wounded I don't think he is very bad has he has not
come to England, I have not received that £7 dear you
promised to send dear, I am sitting in the kitchen and
the sun is pouring in it is a most lovely day, and also
Thursday afternoon just think back and call to mind
what we used to do with ourselves on the very day dear, I
often think of the good times we have had together as
you [k]now I should like to see you all waiting on the
mail, as I expect you are like me never satisfied with all
the letters you get dear like me I had 11 or 12 I don't
know which and the postman remark how many more
do you want quite a lot dear but that is about all you
seem to live on dear. I am sorry to say Harry Evans is a
prisoner of War *[note: the abrupt change of subject here
relates to Tommy]* rough luck with regards to the
operation with his ears and throat dear I am glad it was
done, for it was awful the discharge used to come right
down his little face and smell most horrid, but now there
is nothing of that, and he was the only one out of 30
other children that did not have to be done the second
time and he is better in health for it dear I can tell you,

you ask me if I have got any more money on the
allotment not up till the present we are going to get it
come October and that will be 2/- more which will make
25/- per week, and to start off with they have put them
train fairs [fares] up again and also they have put 3d per
pound on the meat you know that tins of pineapple we
used to buy for 31/2 well thay [they] are 2/6 and 2/9 per
tin the same thing dear, fancy the girls wearing bracelets
right up there arms and legs I wonder if they have got
one there, if they wear clothes they must be more than 4
years old I suppose everything is alright so long as they
cover there [their] ?nappy and if you saw it I suppose
you would think it was in a fit, I have sent the photo but
I don't like them at all I shall be sending some more as I
am having them done dear, by the way do send me your
photo as you promised in shorts dear I am longing to
have a peep at you if only by a picture dear, little Tommy
is very proud of his Father being in India he tells
everybody where you are dear and you are coming home
when the war is over he very much want to go to school
I think I shall let him go dear from morning till night he
keeps on about school I expect it sound rather strange to
you but of course you know he turn 4 years of age and
not slow in any ways dear I am going to write to you
every day except Saturday and Monday so you may keep
on having 6 or 7 letters a week I think it would be a good
idea as it must be rotten for you fellows out there not
getting news of home dear Well dear I must close with
fond love and kisses I remain your darling Lizzie

74 Ossory Road
Old Kent Rd
SE1
London

Aug 20 [1918]
(3)

Dearest
Just a line in answer to your most lovely letter I received
I am so glad you still love me as you do dear for you
know you have been away from me just 11 months dear
and it seem years to me dear I never thought I would
have put up with it but there it is it is a knock out how
do you get over things dear and it has surprised too, Well
dear I am so glad you like writing to me so as it cheer me
up to know that someone is thinking of you when things
don't run smooth dear, but at present they don't never
mind it will not last for ever I am a little downhearted
tonight dear you know the feeling well I espect [expect],
no one seem to want you and it lower your spirit dear
but never mind dear I often think when you were at
home dear and the good time we used to have and the
people used to ask us out to there places some good
evening we have had together dear but now time have
altered no one seem to want you ever your carrie don't
because I wouldnt let her drain me dry, she wants to
grab so much now she is better but she forget it's a
struggle to live for me that don't count, you ask after
Ewart he has got his discharge lucky fellow don't you
think so, you say you are eating bananas, we cannot buy
them hear [here] dear there is none to be had, Tommy
got his handkerchiefs alright dear and his quite please
with them to I never got anything off the post office they
sent me a letter telling me they could not be responsible

for things that came a long way and were breakable, so I
had to let the matter slip dear With regards to the £7 I
have not received it this makes a week and a half from
the time that you wrote and told me you were sending it
by this mail dear, write and explain to me what to do
dear, I am surprise at you wanting a little girl as you do
prehaps [perhaps] it is being a long way from me dear as
you have, had you been at home you might not fill [feel]
that way never mind dear, you fill [feel] you don't care
what you risk if you are both together to share it dear
and I should not mind if I had you at the back of me as
it would not matter so much dear, and the next is a girl
so don't get making a mistake, you say you want her to
be as I was when I was a baby well my mother alway said
I was quite a little tiny mite and a black head of hair
right down my back, and was as good as gold, of course I
cannot account for this at all only I have heard her say so
dear but I cannot answer for those days but I should be
able to answer for the very small as there is not much of
me now dear quite enough for you I suppose, all wont it
be lovely when you come home again as this is quite a
life on one's own dear and I expect you find it the same
as there is no better life than when two people love one
another as we do you don't seem to care a bit and you
can face fire and water for each other dear you must
think of Tommy and myself dear at home waiting for to
meet you again and again dear, how little Tommy long
for the time when you are coming home dear, he often
speak of you as to when you are coming home and how
you will take him out in the tram dear I often show a
little tear when I think of the little pleasure never mind
you can make up all of what he is losing when you come
home dear, you will be thinking this is a rotten letter if I
keep on but I do love you so dear and it hurt me when I
cant get to you never mind I love you and that you love

me and that is a comfort itself dear I must close hoping
you are quite well I remain your darling wife Lizzie

74 Ossory Rd
Old Kent Rd
SE

Aug 25 [1918]

Dearest
Just a line hoping to find you in the pink of health as it
leaves us both at present dear, I received 3 letters
yesterday dear from you which I was pleased to get I can
tell you dear, Well dear you [k]now I have not received
that £7 yet you first said you was sending it on buy [by]
the last post which was three weeks ago, and then I get a
letter asking me if I have received it that letter is dated
12/7/18 and I received it on the 24 of Aug (the letter I
mean not the money) dear up till now I have only got
the £3 you sent not the 7 pounds at all dear so I should
make enquiries about it dear if I was you I went to the
post office and they told me that you would have to see
into it so let me know as soon as possible dear and
should I hear anything of it I will write at once to you,
Well dear I am sending you our George address as you
will know he has been moved again and the address is
(Gunner P.G.Golder 425, 83 RFA RA details G.B.D.
Kantara, Egyptian Expeditionary Force Egypt) I should
think by your letters you have got some ovens out there,
thank goodness they are not like that hear [here] as what
with the price of things and the rotten cooking of the
food I should be fit to give up life, altergether
[altogether], I don't see anything of Fred or Bill at all
dear nor Sid they are earning tons of money and cannot
be bother with the likes of myself dear when you call
they are just going out or are very tired and want to lay
down any excuse so as you do not stop dear you know a
sort of sorry you called way, there I shall not be ready to

make people so comfortable when you come home I can tell you, I am speaking from one that has experience since you have gone I can tell you dear, I am worried very much about that £7 dear do you think you will be able to claim it back I cannot understand it at all, and it was rotten for you to be broke as a rule you are quite the reverse dear, I did get ½ lb of sugar dear and I was very pleased with it to I thought I wrote and told you about it you ask the price of port wine it is 6d a drop and 4 drops go to a quartern thins [things] are very hard here I can tell you and one is at its wits end how to spend the money to the best advantage dear but never mind it cannot last for ever and the sooner the change comes the better for everybody I can tell you, you ask if there was much damage done in Avondale Square it is dreadful a big family wipe out and two houses gone right away dear cannot see anything dear only a lot of rubbish it is the worst night we had I can tell you of course they dropped bombs in the Verey Rd and also in the Rotherhithe New Rd all this end of Kent Rd but thank goodness we have had quite a time in June dear, of course people are beginning to get frighten now we have the harvest moon coming next month that was when we had 7 nights of it 5 or 6 hours gunfire dear last year but I think now that the Government have taken us into hand – people seem to think that they will never get through this barrage they are about to use on them, well dear our Arthur is on 10 days leave and is going to France when he goes back dear no doubt you are surprise dear. I will send you his address as soon as I get it dear, hear [here] I close hoping this war will soon be over and you will be home soon I remain your loving wife

Lizzie

74 Ossory Road
Old Kent Road

Undated [August 1918]

Dearest

Just a note hoping you are quite well as it leaves Tommy
and myself much better than we have been Well dear I
got the £7 which I thank you very much dear for Well
dear I have had to go away for a holiday as I am very ill I
am on the verge of a breakdown dear Well dear don't
worry about me, I can tell you what I am very lonely at
home and I am fed up with everything dear, my work is
not going so smooth as it was dear and of course as you
know things in London are very trying dear, I am sick
and tired of everything dear I have written to Southend
and I am waiting a reply dear, But I don't know if I will
get fixed up dear Well dear I do hope and trust you will
be home soon dear as this life cannot go on like this dear
Well I am going to bed feeling quite misable [miserable]
tonight dear I now close hoping you the best of luck I
remain your loving wife Lizzie

74 Ossory Rd
Old Kent Rd
SE1

Aug 28th [1918]

Dearest
Just a line to let you know I have received the £7 and
have put it in the bank I put £13-10 £7 you sent and the
rest I had saved dear I don't think I am so bad at times I
think your sisters get jealous of me, I think that is what
is the matter with pops as I happened to tell her I had
got money in the bank, I should think they ought to be
please as you could have done worse, look at your
brother George's wife, he as [has] been home on 3 week
leave the same old tale up to her eyes in debt and he has
bought her a very thick heavy bracelet gold of course,
the excuse pops gave for her is she must see life she
could not sit at home moping must be out and about a
very poor excuse I think getting her husband in debt just
for enjoying herself, instead of turning out to work like
other people and keeping herself straight, them kind of
people seem all in all to pops I can't understand her at
all dear, Well dear I received 3 letters from you this week
just think that makes 14 just lately dear and I am very
please to think you are thinking of us so they filled up an
empty mind at times the only thing is it make one
greedy you seem to look for more still, Well dear I have
got something tell you old Murry has got kick[ed] out of
the insurance has got rumble at last caught napping this
time dear, it wont surprise you I don't suppose as all
rough have got to come to it sooner or later dear I know
you will be pleased to hear about it I am I can tell you, as
he did not care for us when we got married did he, you
know I felt that very much dear although I did not show

it but I was always shur [sure] it was him who done his best for us at that time Well dear I am pleased you are going on alright and learning working well dear I shall get you to do the cooking I shall take it easy when you come home dear, I have made a rabbit pie dear today and it is lovely I should have like[d] you to be hear [here] and had dinner with us I know you would have enjoy[ed] it dear well dear it is getting late and I shall be going to bed hear [here] I close I remain your loving wife Lizzie

74 Ossory Rd
Old Kent Rd

Sept 5th [1918]

Dearest
Just a line hoping you are in the pink of health as it
leaves us both at present dear Well dear our Arthur will
not go to France until he is 19 a new order has come out
to say all those that are in England are not to go to
France until they are 19, Well dear the war is going on
alright now by the read of the papers dear and I should
thing [think] were coming to an end dear if you can go
by the papers, I am please you are getting my letters now
as it must be very miserable for you as what I can see of
your own people they do not write you but never mind
when you come home you will have to give them the go
by the same way as they are serving you now dear, I have
been thinking when you do come home I shall move
right away from all of them as they are all as bad as
another it's the old saying when you have got your old
man by you everything go well, but when he has gone
you should not be living but never mind dear when you
come home, and please God it wont be long now I hope,
as I am fed up with this sort of life and I expect you are
the same dear, I should like a nice little flat with my own
street door and no one use it but us wouldn't it be nice
dear no one to interfere with you and do as you like, I
should so much like that better than where I am now
dear I am really bent on one dear and when you come
home do hope you will like it to[o], they are a little more
rent, but they are worth it and if it was not for the
moving alone I should take one now dear as the
conveniences are much better dear than where we are
now, old Squibbs has got a little bungalow 3 miles from

the station the only house for miles around got 60 chickens dear as happy as the days were long she would not come back to London for anything, Well dear got the £7 alright after worrying about it and I put it in the bank I [k]now you would be pleased when you come home with the bank dear I have done my best dear, I should think you have got a fine time with bugs out there I should think that the people are very dirty out there thank goodness we have had no more raids since that one in Avondale Square and don't want any more I can tell you, old Tom is getting a fine big boy I can tell you he keep on about going to school dear I think he will learn quickly as he has got everything taped I can tell you and if you come home tomorrow you wont be surprised at him put to bed at 6o/c and you don't hear anymore of him till the next morning he look fat and healthy I can tell you, would be proud of him I [k]now if only you could see him go to the shop for different little things I want and bring them right to[o], none of that carrying on as we used to have with him I have broken him in of all that you would be surprised at him I [k]now, I have being doing the front room out today and it look a little picture I only thought if only you could come in now you would think it looked lovely dear, this week I have been very busy like I use to get ready when you were coming home from Tonbridge Wells dear how I used to hurry up with my work so you had it nice and comfortable for you I often wonder if you will come home when I least expect you I wish it was soon I can tell you dear, Well dear I must close with fondest love and kisses

I remain your loving
Wife Lizzie

74 Ossory Rd
Old Kent Rd

Sept 13 [1918]

Dearest
Just a line hoping you are feeling quite well as it leaves us
at present Well dear I am rather upset over you saying
you are only going to write me 1 letter a month dear I
am sorry I did not send you very regular but I have been
very queer in myself dear, I am still under the doctor he
said I am amicae [?anaemic] and you may guess how I
feel dear what with you away and then being so queer
but never mind I am much better than I have been, we
have got £75-17-10 in the bank I have received another
£1 from you dear, Well dear you ask me if I have time to
think, it would not do for me to think as there is not
much good for me to think dear for the more I think the
more lonely I feel, Well dear I have thought of you a
great deal this week I cannot understand only having
one letter with this mail, you know I do my best at
home, I cannot think what makes you so very cold in
your one letter received this mail, I have been thinking
perhaps you have got that letter telling you about Carrie
and you have turned nasty over it, but I think it was my
place to stick up for the boy, the same as she would do if
it was her kids but I have and [you] are thinking ill of
me I cannot help it, there is one thing I shall not go and
see any of them when you come home you may please
yourself what you do I am sick of both side and please
God to spare you to come back I shall move right away
out of it, away from all of them so they shall not now
[know] everything that goes on and life would not hold
much for me then, I hope you are getting my letters
better now as you should do dear, and we have not had

any air raids dear this last month, little Tommy is going
on alright and is in the best of health dear

Well dear write me as soon as I do miss your letters hear
[here] I close I remain your loving wife
Lizzie

74 Ossory Road
Old Kent Road

Sept 18 [1918]

Dearest
Just a line hoping to find you in the pink of health as it
leaves us at present, Well dear I have got some very bad
news my brother Jack has been killed dear on the 5th of
Sept it is most awful when you come to look at it left
those 4 kiddies and God know what will become of
them dear they had the news through so it is quite right
dear Well dear when you think of poor old Jack and
what he has gone through, you are the best off dear, it
has upset me very much and I have thought how awful it
must be to be brought to your door like poor old nell
has had it, I am very very sorry dear I will write and let
you know more if I get it at all Well dear I do love you so
sometimes I feel I should like to fly over if I could dear
of course this life is very dispressing [depressing] with
one thing and another, All I hope dear it will not be long
before this wicked war is over and done with if only to
save the lives of the poor young fellows how [who] are
paying dearly with their young life through no fault of
there own, and the worse of all is being taken away from
there wives and children it is a most alful [awful] crime
dear and when you look into things it appear worse.
Well dear are you still at the same place I hope you stop
there as I think you appear to be much better off and if
you want to get your discharge I think it best for you
there for if they sent you home you might have to go to
France and then it would be a sorce [source] of worry
dear to me as if anything happen I lose all dear not that I
am ashamed of what I do as there is nothing to be
ashamed of I hope by the time you get this letter you

have got my letters and you are not so offish with me

Hear [here]I close hoping you are in the best of health I remain your loving wife Lizzie

PS I am glad you like the photo they are not so nice as they should be, but I am going to have some more done in a couple of weeks and will send you one of them

PS I have been dreaming of you all the week dear

74 Ossory Rd
Old Kent Rd

Sept 20 [1918]

Dearest
Just a line hoping you are quite well as it leaves us at
present, Well dear I do hope and trust you are still going
well and at the same place for as you say they are going
to France from where you are stopping I think it must be
very trying in [illegible? France] it is very sad about poor
Jack as those kids of his are very young it is a shame he
has been very unlucky Well dear I have had my fortune
told and it is very curious the woman told me I should
hear of a death of a dark man and it concerns the family
and she has told me that you were very fond of us and
was always thinking of us at home she said you were
coming home soon which I hope is quite true [illegible]
will not be long before you do come as I do love you so
and I want so much God knows I do want you a lot but
after all we have been very lucky as if you continue till
the end of the war I think we shall not have much to
grumble at, Our stays have gone up 2 shillings on every
pair so I expect it will fall a bit flat owing to the diffrence
in prices dear Well dear I expect you find it very trying
dear I expect you miss us very much but is only natural
[several lines illegible] Well dear Tommy has just said he
don't want the ears he has got he want rabbits ears so if
you should come across a pair of them kindly send them
home for him Ollidge Parsons Green Well dear I think
the way the kid is coming along he will be a lad he is
always full of fun I know you would be pleased to hear
him at times I can tell you Well dear I close hoping to
hear from you soon I remain your loving wife

74 Ossory Rd
Old Kent Rd

Sept 22nd [1918]

Dearest
Just a line hoping you are quite well as it leaves both at
present dear I am very sorry for Nell as she has got those
4 kiddies and things are very dear, you don't say if you
understand my letters or not I should like to know if
they are alright, as you complained about the writing
and spelling so let me know if it is better Well dear as
you know we have ration books to get what food we
want and it is a lark I can tell you we are waiting for new
ones now as the others are full up, but it is ever so much
better we do get a bit where before we use to line up and
then chance weather [whether] we got it or not but we
do get some now dear no[t] much but there it is dear I
am glad you like the photo dear Well dear I cannot write
as I have not got much to say, our stays have gone up 2
or more on every pair that makes 11-11 the cheapest so
it has made a bit of a difference to us you can bet but
never mind dear we shall get over that by the way the
war is going on I think we shall be alright for Christmas
as I think all the fighting will be done dear don't you
think so lets hope it is so as the suffering to poor people
is to[o] great for words dear what with mothers having
there sons taken and likewise the wives having there
husbands taken there seem we shall have no ending dear,
Wont we have a lot to make up for dear I shall be glad
when the times come that you come home dear to us
both and then we shall be happy again wont we dear just
you think dear sitting besides the kitchen fire like we
used to do dear, I have got a nice fire today just the sort
you used to like it is very cold the weather is now dear

and of course it is pleasant with a fire I can tell you I
expect you forget how a fire looks as that is the thing you
don't see I suppose Well dear I hope you will be in the
pink of health as it leaves us both at present I now close
with fondest love and kisses I remain your loving wife

Lizzie

PS Tommy send his love and kisses he is getting a big
boy I can tell you no baby ways at all I should like you to
see him

74 Ossory Rd
Old Kent Rd

Sept 29 [1918]

Dearie
Just a line in answer to your letter which I received Sept
28th I am so sorry to hear you are in hospital I do hope
you are better by the time you received this letter, do you
think they will get you glasses, but there you had better
be in India than in France, how things are going out
there now dear, they have got the news from the War
office about Jack he was killed on the 5th Sept rotten
luck for those how [who] are left dear, there is £1-5
owing on the piano dear so that wont be long before it is
paid for, I don't think if I were you dear I should not put
anything in the bank as the post office is the best. We are
having some rotten weather here rain rain every day
gives me the pip I can tell you, with regards to Bert I
have not seen him since he had my two bob. I don't
think India seem to agree with you dear as you are
always queer, I hope they give you your ticket play up for
it if you can old dear, your Bob is not married yet, and I
have not seen anything of them as I don't go round there
at all, I shall not go there any more as Carrie has treated
me very mean, it seem as soon as she knew I had saved a
shilling she was jealus [jealous], I think it run in the
family a bit with the girls especially because when she
knew I had got it in the bank she carried on because it
was in your name, she wanted me to draw it out and go
to Brighton and I could see through it afterwards she
was going down there to earn the money and I was
going to be the lackey and earn nothing but do all the
rough work for her and that was the real state of the
case, so if you think I have done roung [wrong] I don't,

the two kids of hers are perfect little buggers you are
alright as long as keep giving them pennies but that cant
always come off, and I tell you if you don't stick up for
yourself in these days people take liberties with you well
dear my work is very quite [quiet] at present but it go up
and down a lot

Well dear I must now close hoping you are in the best of
health when you received this letter hear [here] I close I
remain your loving wife Lizzie

74 Ossory Road
Old Kent Road

Oct 2 [1918]

Dearest
Just a line hoping you are better and are getting about
again Well dear I am very pleased with the war I should
think it could not last much longer than another month
dear I read that the Germans want peace terms or
re[bellion] will take place out there we have got right
through Cambria grand news dear I think I shall see you
now before Christmas dear all what a meeting dear,
wont it be, I am so sick of this life dear what with one
thing and another the people upstairs are going to move
dear just because the rain is coming in the roof I tell you
we have to go something to put up with so when you
come home I want you to take me out of it altogether a
nice new flat on our own with your own street door I
should be quite satisfied you (k)now dear this house has
been a real worry to me since we have been there as he
will not have the roofings done properly keeps patching
them up it sickening but I will put up with it till you
come home and then I will get you to settle me
somewhere else the real facts is that the roofing is rotten
and won't stand the rain at all, so dear you must make it
up to me when you come home dear that is all dear I do
hope they make people comfortable when they come I
will let you know what next lot I get in dear they seem to
come in alright and then get dissatisfied I cannot
understand some people dear,

Well dear I must now close hoping you are going alright dear

I remain your loving wife Lizzie

74 Ossory Rd
Old Kent Rd

Oct 5 [1918]

Dearest
Just a line hoping you are going on alright dear Well I
really don't know what to put in this letter, only I do
wish this war was over dear so as you were home dear
sometimes I feel very lonley [lonely] dear I do tonight
and very downhearted too I do not go out much
perhaps that is what it is dear but there is not much to
go out for the streets are very dark, and if you go to the
pictures they close early dear owing to the gas and coal
business, well all I can say is everybody has got the hump
and the sooner the war is over the better for everyone
dear, I am very sorry, little Nellie is very ill the shock of
her father dear dear as I expect you have got the news by
now dear it is most sad and those dear little kiddies
being left like that all I can say he was one of the best of
fathers and thought the world of his children to[o],
Christmas is coming near now and I wonder if it will be
peaceful if only the fighting was over I think it cannot
last much longer dear do you think so, I see in todays
paper that the Germans are asking for peace terms I am
afraid they wont get it dear as it must be won now dear
at all cost and we have to give up a lot of lives yet dear I
can tell you it is awful is it not just you think of the poor
fellows that have been killed dear in this war it is quite
distressing to think of, Well dear I am not getting many
letters from you only 4 by these last two mails dear, have
you not been well enough to write me or are you cross in
any way with me dear, I suppose I am [greedy] I have
been used to having 5 or 6 the mail the [that] came in
on Aug I got 12 letters so I expect I think I ought to have

more, so do write as much as you can dear as I do look
forward for letters dear Well dear I must close hoping
you are going on alright I remain your loving wife Lizzie
and love from little Tommy

74 Ossory Road
Old Kent Rd

Oct 9 [1918]

Dearest
Just a line hoping to find you in the best of health as it
leaves us both at present dear Well dear I have got a little
bit more trouble the people in the house a[re] moving
because the rain come in so in the kitchen I have seen
Mr Laham about it and he said that he cannot get any
men to do repairs, the roof has got to be stripped, be
[but] he is very kind he said he cannot help it, he has
said he will only take my rent that would be 6/- until I
have got the roof done and let again, it is a dame job
what with no men at home the Landlord said himself if
he can get a man to do the job he will dear so don't you
worry about it, I expect it will turn out alright but it is
trouble dear I can tell you We must keep on smiling as
the war cannot last much longer dear do you think it
can, I think it will soon come to a close now, and I know
you will be pleased if only to come home to help me
with a little bit worry off my mind dear as you know
these houses are in a bad state with regards to the
roofings every tenant speaks of the way the rain and the
Landlord (k)now himself how they are and he admits
they are the worst houses he has got regards to the roofs
he told me that it would cost £75 to re roof every house
and the trustees wont pay it, of course the party in the
house was rather bugged, she stops paying her rent and
told me she would not pay anymore until the roof was
done so I went after her you can bet I don't care
stoppage is no payment so I gave her my mind and told
her she would have to go, she is one of these swankers,
her husband works in the ars[e]nal earning all the

money and you bet how they swank about but I took the
wind out of her sails when I told her to go I can tell you,
I have let them again and the people are coming in next
week, they are a young couple with a baby 1 year old
dear he works on the railway I think they are very nice
what I know of them dear and there is no reason why we
should not be happy all together, of course this party
how [who] is going has got a boy 10 years and he is a
perfect bugger I cannot keep the place clean for he wont
whip [wipe] his feet and most cheeky I can tell you, so I
shall not be sorry to see the back of them, she said it is
not her boy, put all the blame on my Tommy so you can
bet it pleases me never mind I have to let you know all
this so as you can see how things are dear but don't
worry about me as I can take my own part dear, I have
made her part up with the rent alright up to now of
course she is going this week and leave it to me to get
this week rent alright, Well dear I must close and will let
you know how things go with us dear latter [later]

I remain your loving wife Lizzie

74 Ossory Rd
Old Kent Rd

Oct 17 [1918]

Dearest
Just a note to let you know we are going on alright dear I
have got 5 letter by this mail, I am so sorry to hear you
are so queer dear but I hope by the time you get this
letter you will be much better dear with regards to the
Spanish flue, it is awful hear [here] people are dying off
like flies, Well dear I do see life in 74 Ossory Road I can
tell you I have got some more lodgers in now they seem
very nice they go to church on Sunday, and I don't mind
that I can tell you I suppose you wonder why the other
people have moved well I am sorry to say they wanted
the house for there 8/- so I had to have a row and nearly
chuck them out but all well that end well I can tell you, it
really started like this, the rain came in the kitchen
sealing [ceiling], and she had the cheek to come down
and tell me she would not pay any more rent before the
roof was done so I said if was not done in a month or six
month I suppose you wont pay until then and she said
no, so I gave her a week notice to get out, she said I shall
go when I like so she gave me the trouble of 3 week to get
her out but I have got rid of her and got my rent has [as]
well, and these I have made pay a week in advance which
is 8/- so I don't think I have done bad dear, I am like little
Tommy and his song don't cryee 52 [?] Gothas in the
skyee Well dear I will write you another letter in a day or
so as I am very tired and it is late dear hear [here] I close
wishing you the best of luck I remain your loving wife

Lizzie

74 Ossory Rd
Old Kent Rd
SE1

[undated] [from context late October 1918]

Dearest
Just a line in answer to your letter, Well dear I am so
sorry to hear you are so ill I don't think India agree with
you dear, but hang on as much as you can as I don't
think this war is going to last very long dear as the news
is great and it make one think it cannot last over
Christmas although you feel sad when you think of
though [those] who have been killed dear I and [am]
sorry for one and all how [who] have lost anybody in
this dreadful war as God know it will be alful [awful] for
the poor dear waiting, and no return for there wait dear,
Well dear I must change the subject as it makes me so
upset dear, I have put 2£ in the bank we have got
£81.17.10 I am Afraid I shall not get a hundred by
Christmas dear I will do my best but it want getting
nearly £20 by that time and only eight week to do it dear
I should have be[en] able to put in another 10/- but I
have 3 pairs of boots soled and 2 pairs of shoes for
Tommy done this week that cost me 9 shillings 7d for
repairs if you were at home I should not have that to pay
for dear but never mind I still have hope of meeting you
again dear and that is what a lot of poor creatures will
not have dear, which I feel very sorry for and everybody
thinks there own is the best dear don't they, Well dear
what do you think of the good news in the papers I
expect you gat [get] to [k]now as we do everybody about
hear [here] are ever so glad it is quite a change to what
we have been having we are going to get more money
from 1st October dear I shall get 2/6 more that makes

25/6 per week dear not much considering the way the
food has gone up again dear, we have been troubled a lot
with the strike dear and there has been no buses running
for over a week, then the tubes were closed and several
other trades have been striking so you guess it has been
very funny here, but things have settled down a bit for a
time I expect until someone else find the money is not
enough Well dear I hope it will not be long before you
are home with us again dear With Gods will and wishes
and pray it will not be any more wars as we are all fed up
with them hear [here] I close hoping to see you soon I
remain your loving wife Lizzie

74 Ossory Rd
Old Kent Rd

Nov 3rd [1918]

Dearest
Just a line hoping you are in the best of health as it leaves
us at present Well dear I received 3 letters by the mail all
very nice ones, only to[o] much work about them, you
know I am just about fed up with work and I don't mind
telling you, I am order by the doctor to take 3 months
rest at the very least I have got my old complaint come
back to me, I fell right down ill I don't (k)now how to
explain it to you dear, I wish this war was over and you
were coming home I should get you to take a place in the
country for a time dear I fell [feel] that is just the kind of
thing that would do me any good at all dear, of course
you understand I have had a lot to put up with since you
have been away what with the house and the lodgers, in
and out things have not been all honey here I can tell
you, what I see of the lodger they expect you to stop at
home and nurse them, when you go to work they are as
static as you like I get the perfect sick of lodgers they
seem to think you are letting to oblige them, when you
come home I shall take a place to myself dear and then
only have your own dirt to clear up not be servant for
others in the house and that is what it amount to dear I
think you earn that 2 shilling in keeping the place clean
also the ware and tare [wear and tear] of the passage
dear, no doubt you will wonder at this letter, but I am
sick of keeping house dear, I have got some more people
in they seem alright, but you don't (k)no(w) any one
dear, anyway there is a long time before us dear and I
might feel better when you come home and then we
could make arrangements then for the future dear, I am

not cross with you dear, only this long waiting seem
years dear and it worry one to death at time, as it seem
as if you are never coming home dear, but there I am
rather downhearted today the weather has been very bad
this week and it is pouring of rain all day, and the
kitchen is very low, and of course it is very depressing
dear to[o] one [? how] does not make any friends but I
must not worry you and I hope and trust that it will not
be long before all will be at an end and then you will be
at home with us and make us happy again dear, as I
expect you get the same sort of feeling as I do you want
us badly, and I feel I cannot live much longer without
seeing you dear Well dear I close hoping you are getting
better I remain your loving wife Lizzie

74 Ossory Rd
Old Kent Rd

[undated] [Early November 1918]

Well Dearie
Just a line to let you [k]now how pleased I am with
myself dear I think we shall soon have peace now, I feel
so pleased I could dance on my head with my legs up in
the air, as you know the Austrians have surrendered so I
don't think Germany will hold out much longer now
dear do you, fancy dear you will not be long before you
are home to us again dear if it pleases God which I do
pray for, just to have you home again dear, as you
[k]now life is very blank without you dear, and I expect
you fill [feel] just the same towards us, I now [no] doubt
you would like to be with us dear, I expect you cannot
make yourself contented dear but never mind I still love
you and I have still got a nice home for you to come
back to us and Tommy is getting such a big boy you
won't [k]now him dear there is no baby ways about him
dear I can tell you, I fill [feel] sure you would be surprised
at him he is quite the father to me and look after me as
well I can tell you dear. Well dear up to the present I am
very comfortable with the people upstairs as you know I
have got rid of the others as they had too much old buck
I can tell you but these are very nice up to now and I
think they will be alright to me as they seem very sorry
for me having you away as you are and having to carry
on in the same way as if you were at home dear and
having to be mother and father too they go to church
but that make no difference to me as I had better have
that than drink dear there is nothing to be ashamed of at
living a good life and I don't know that I shall be the
same as I don't think you can do better, they have got

such a pretty little baby with lovely curly hair Well dear I don't know what to put in your letter at times it puzzle me but never mind I think I shall soon have you home the way things are going with the war dear as it cannot last much longer there is splendid news this week and the war cannot go much longer now I shouldn't so as our people are paying them right and left I think they will give in at the end of it all as they have suffered very badly this last 2 weeks but there is no telling what will happen yet dear, Well dear I must close hoping you are going on much better I remain your loving wife Lizzie

74 Ossory Rd
Old Kent Rd

[undated] – [just after Armistice 1918}

Dearest
Just a line to let you [k]now we are going on alright and
feeling more ourselves, well dear we had a very bad
attack of the flue and Tommy had Bronc[h]itis with his
so you can bet we had our share dear, Well dear what do
you think of the war being over dear, I hear that the
firms are going to clame [claim] the men so I have been
thinking if Mr Bever [? Beber] will be put for you dear, I
have been told that if I go and see him he might do his
best dear so I am going tomorrow, an[d] I will let you
know what he says dear, I [k]now there is a lot of people
doing the same thing, and he speaks well of you dear so
there is no reason why he should not do his best for you
dear, I think it is a[s] good as over the war I mean dear,
thank God, things have been most alful [awful] dear of
late, this loneliness is unbearable of late dear I can tell
you, I have had my fortune told and things are most true
everything has come true she told me about our Jack,
and lot more things dear and they have come true she
told me you will be coming home soon I do hope that
will come true to[o] Well dear I am going to do my best
I think I shall be able to talk to him dear, Well dear little
Tommy is getting a monkey, have had to buy a cane for
him right out of hand I can tell you, he wont let me get
up in the morning said I want to love you something
[illegible] put up with isn't it dear the piano is paid for
dear, so we shall have a smooth run when you do come
home dear I feel shur [sure] that you will [be] please[d]
with your home dear I have keep things running just as
if you were at home dear so I don't think you will have

much to grumble at dear, it has been a struggle at time[s], when you have got to buy a Jarcey [?jersey] and have to pay 7/6 for it only Tommy size and 11/3 for his shoes nothing cheaper dear I can tell you, I have got to buy him some new shirts the flannette [?flannelette] is 2/3 per yard and it takes 3/ yards to make 2 shirts so you may guess what it cost to live dear, we don't get any more food, and now we are ration[ed] for jam I cannot get any for 8 weeks they are only serving it in 2lb pots, we are allowed 4 ozs a week but they wont sell it in 4/ozs so we have got to wait for 8 weeks before we get our supply not so bad is it I get sick of it at time I can tell you dear

Well dear this nib is so rotten and we cant get any blotting paper, so I do hope you will be able to understand this letter hear [here] I close I remain your loving wife Lizzie

74 Ossory Rd
Old Kent Rd

[undated] [late 1918]

Dearest old Tom

Just a line hoping you don't think I am dead I have not
written to you for a fortnight owing to me and Tommy
being ill in bed with the flu we are much better now but
it has left my nerve very bad as you will see by the
writing dear but the doctor said I shall go along alright if
I take care of myself which I intend to do as I can dear.
Tommy has got up very much run down dear, I am
giving him Scott Emulsion and with care I think he will
be alright in a few week dear, we are lucky to have got
about again as there is five people died in the street with
the flue dear, I do hope you are alright dear, while I was
in bed I received a letter from you dear nice one to[o] it
was so nice for I was miserable lying there, and it come a
God send to me I can tell you, we had to stop in bed a
week so you can bet we were pretty bad dear well dear I
have got some bad news for you old Squibbs has lost her
husband he died with the flu, been dead a week today I
am truly sorry for her dear as she is the best of girls dear,
Well dear the war is over, I wonder when you will be
coming home dear, I do want to see you so much I can
tell you, and little Tommy is looking forward for your
coming dear, I [k]now you don't want to come home it
is only a buzz, but it is hard to be parted dear don't you
think so but there we have been lucky for we have got
the chance of meeting [one] another again dear and
many have got there hopes smach [smashed] there is
Jack['s] little children for one I think it is so sad when
you look into things dear, I get quite chock [?choked]

but never mind we must live for [one] another and then
we shall still love [one] another, for we do love each
other so much as it make one sad at time don't it dear, I
love you so much that I fill [feel] I cannot wait much
longer for you but I think the worse is over now and we
will have a good time before us dear which I am looking
forward for and with God help we shall be happy again
dear, I have not paid Carrie that 12/6 yet and I don't
intend to I can tell you dear I think she treated me most
dirty don't you think I am surprise [at] her I can tell
you, I am done with the whole of the lot, and when you
come home we shall live for one another dear that will
be the best, as I can see you[r] people are jealus
[jealous], and my people are the same so they can go and
hang thereself [themselves] as I am done with both
sides, and you will find it quite the best, as you will see
for yourself that what I say is true dear jealousness is at
the bottom of both sides but let the[m] get on with it I
am finished with trying to please people I can tell you
they don't mind how they hurt your feelings, but you
must not hurt there[s] [theirs], that is the world of
today, but hang them all, I am pushing on alright
without them and they can get on with it dear, I am now
waiting to see you, you are the only one I cannot get on
without you dear, I don't know why but there it is, life is
not worth living at times I can tell you work and worry
that is all it amount[s] to but never mind we are very
lucky dear as I have said before, and it is a long lane
without any turning so they say, and I think we are at the
turn now dear as things are much brighter than they
have been, Well dear I am just going to bed to dream of
you as I very often do dear you are always in my
thoughts in my mind and also in my dreams I am always
thinking of you dear and I [k]now you return it dear,

well goodnight hear [here] I close hoping it will not be
long before you are home again

I remain your loving wife Lizzie

74 Ossory Rd
Old Kent Rd

[undated] [from context late November 1918]
[incomplete]

Dearest
You must excuse me for not writing before, but we have
both been very ill with the flue, little Tommy has been
very bad indeed I got very frighten[ed] of him I can tell
you, there are ever so many people dying hear [here]
with it I had 2 letters with this mail dear I am very sorry
you have been ill with the flue, I say don't you feel rotten
I have not got over my packet at all, I feel worse than
when I got up with Tommy and God knows how I felt
then, well dear the war is over do you think you will be
coming home to us soon dear I do hope it will not be
long as I do want you home so, for I seem to find it more
a struggle every week to keep up against it, for one thing
the food is such a trouble to get and the clothes is so
dear and you don't seem to have enough to manage on
dear, I don't mean to worry you dear but if you were
home things would be lighter, for I am fed up and I
[k]now you must be, dear, We are a soppy pair, one cant
do without the other so the sooner they let you come
home the better for the both of us dear what do you
think about it, Well dear the piano is paid up the war is
over and things are looking brighter dear the only thing
I want now is you home with…

74 Ossory Rd
Old Kent Road

Dec 3rd [1918]

Dearest
Just a line to let you [k]now we are going on alright and
hoping it will not be long before you will be home with
us again as I think that by the new year you will be with
us, again dear I expect you are excited over the news we
have heard dear which is most comforting to me, you
will soon be home and that is everything dear, I am only
sorry for one thing and this is because I have promised
you, that you could have a girl, but perhaps you will
forgive me for once as I don't fancy my luck, so I should
tare [tear] this piece of paper up and wait till you come
home and see what mode [mood] you catch me in, as
you know, you are artful you sort of, hit a poor woman
when she is down and that is why you are saving those
pieces of paper, so as to catch me bending O [no] know,
but never mind so long as you keep it to yourself I
expect by this time it is getting more than you can
manage, but you tuck it in your trousers and then it will
fade away, I expect I shall have to go through it when
you come home but never mind I shall stick up for
myself don't worry, well dear how do you like having the
flue a bit rotten don't you think I myself have had two
lots of it and it has left me very queer, I have not got
much go in me, but I suppose you will manage that for
me when you come home dear as I expect you must have
all the go in by now no work to do what is better I
should think you are having a fine time dear, but take
care of everything as I shall have a good look at it when
you come home dear, by the way little Tommy is getting
a fine boy and want you to fetch a little sister home from

India, but I don't quite fancy having a black baby but there we will see what can be done when we meet, I cannot tell you if Bob is married I have only seen him once, and he was with Bill Tyson, and he was afraid to speak to me, as for Arthur he is still in England thank goodness, of course you [k]now by now that poor old Jack is gone, Well dear up to now there is £86 in the bank dear so things are still going alright at home dear, so you need not worry about us at all so far as thing[s] go dear, the only things is I want you with us so and I am bound to feel like that, but we have got better hopes now of see[ing] each other than we have had dear don't you think so, Well dear it is a week to Christmas, I don't suppose for a minute that you will be home with us until the new year but never mind, we have got hopes thank goodness. Well dear I still love you so and I sometime dream of you which are so true I also feel you cuddling me so tight that when I wake up I get quite wild with myself dear but never mind I have got a lot to come dear, which I hope will not be long dear Well dear I must close hoping you are getting better I remain

your loving wife Lizzie

74 Ossory Rd
Old Kent Rd

[undated] [from context December 1918]

Dearest
You must excuse me not writing before it is a week since
I wrote to you but I am very sorry I have got such a bad
foot, the doctor said he thought I should have to go
under an operation but I cannot tell you for certain I
have got an inflamed corn right on the bottom of my
foot and the pain is most awful, I don't know what to do
with it the foot swells dreadful and I cannot get my boot
on at times dear I have to use a lotion to keep the
swelling down, the doctor said it was the walking that is
doing it I am sorry because I am getting on so well I did
not want to give my job up as the money is so sweet and
you cannot find jobs like mine every week dear, well I
have got that £10 dear, and as for the one pound you are
speaking about I got that too but I have written and told
you so you know I have because I got it soon after the £7
dear well it is just a week and 2 days to Christmas
another I wonder how many more holidays we shall have
without one another perhaps now the war is over you
will be home which I hope and trust will not be long
dear as it seem so long ago since I last saw you dear, and
I expect you are as anxious to see us dear so we quite
understand the feeling dear which at times you seem not
to be able to stand dear any more waiting but there it has
been a long struggle for both of us and we have stuck it
well take things all round well dear I have asked Mr
Beber about you and he has wrote a letter to head office
I saw the reply to it they said at present only key men
were being relieved but as soon as the[y] [start]ing
relieving the others you would be the first to be sent for

dear so that is rather nice to [k]now dear, I think if you were at home I should be much better in health dear, but there we will see when you come home how is the doctor dear. As for Tommy he has had a dreadful cold, but is going great now dear, I took him to Selfridges to see the Christmas toys and he was delighted with them there was a nice band there and we had a fine afternoon, had it not been for my foot dear, but I did my best for him I can tell you, so he has to let him enjoy himself dear too toys are a dreadful price and you can bet yourself that Tom wanted everything he see buy me this and that I had a good time before me dear but never mind I did not mind so long as he enjoy it dear,

Well dear I must close as I have got to spend ½ hour on my foot and it is rather late so dear

I remain your loving wife Lizzie

74 Ossory Road
Old Kent Rd

Dec 26th [1918]

Dearest
Just a line hoping to find you in the best of health as it
leaves us at present, Well dear Christmas is over and a
good job to[o], for I don't like the holidays a bit lately
they are very lonely I can tell you, I shall be very glad
when you come home now as I am looking forward for a
good time dear and I should think you will be coming
home soon dear don't you think so, little Tommy has
enjoyed himself this Christmas very much, because he
look[s] forward for father Christmas, and when he woke
up Christmas morning and found he had been his little
face was full of delight to see what he had left him it was
quite pleasing I can tell you, as now is about the age for
him to get interesting in anything of that sort dear, he
could not understand why he had not left me anything,
but I told him mothers don't have anything for there
[their] stocking, Well dear the weather is very cold, I
should not be surprised if we don't have some snow
soon dear, quite frosty, a proper old Christmas I can tell
you, Well dear I had a nice Christmas card from Edie,
the only one that see[ms] to think of us I did think it so
kind of her dear such kind words on it, I think old
George could have done much worst for Edie seem[s] a
very good girl dear and I am pleased to see it I can tell
you have got a nice home for him when he comes home
and that is a lot, as some of these wives as they call
thereselves are leading a nice life I can tell you Well dear
I suppose you are hoping to get home again to us and I
am hoping to see you dear, I don't think it will be long
before we are together again then you will have to mind

your p,a,q, [Ps and Qs] I can tell you no making babies as soon as you are home as I shall be getting wild, be like Mr Asquith wait and see keep on waiting and seeing that's the best dear, I suppose you dream of us and think of us a lot, I do you dear I often dream you are in bed with me to cuddle me nothing nasty just cuddling me so tight that I could not breathe at times dear, I often get wild when I wake up and find it['s] only a dream but never mind I hope it will happen in reality before long dear, only the waiting is so weary dear, ones get so sick at times but is a long lane that has not got a turning for us both dear with God's will and everything is [? plotted] out in life for all so we must be patient and then we will have all in good time at God's will Well dear I do hope you are keeping well and we are doing alright up to the present so don't worry over us dear I must close hoping to hear from you soon I remain your loving wife Lizzie

Love from little Tommy

[small envelope, empty, but with Lizzie's writing on face]
[Christmas card for 1918]

Little Tommy think[s] if he send[s] this P.C with the
train you will get home much quicker not a bad judge is
he like the rest fed up with all of it dear he pick[ed] the
card out at the shop to send to you dear
Love Lizzie

1919

74 Ossory Rd
Old Kent Rd

Jan 12th [1919]

Dearest
Just a line hoping to find you in the best of health as it
leaves us at present Well dear I have had 4 nice letters
this mail dear I am pleased you are better than you have
been dear, I expect you will be short of some of my
letters as I have not been writing just lately dear I have
only wrote 3 in a month that is because I have been very
queer, yes I really thought I should have to give up
altogether, I have had a lot of time off just lately but Mr
Savage has been very good he has keep [kept] my job
open, dear I think I shall have quite a job to leave when I
want to, has [as] he will not hear of me giving up in any
way, of course the book I have now is £17, and when I
took it over it was only 4-12 and that is the Walworth
Road round it is getting as much as I can manage I can
tell you, of course if I give up I should not be able to
manage on my army money because the things are so
dear that you could not manage it would be no good I
can tell you, Well dear I am glad to thing [think] that
you will be home some time this year, I hope it will be
soon dear as I think they could hurry this afare [affair]
on[so] much quicker if they try, I think the soldiers
ought to make a fuss about it and then that might do a
bit of good the men that are still in England and have
never been overseas seem to be getting there tickets
without any trouble at all the [?men] that waited for
there papers not the men that volunteered I have got the
£10 dear 2 week before Christmas so that is alright dear
Tom said when he join up he think he will go to India
not France because you don't get killed in India no[t] a

bad judge is he, I have bought him a pair of boots youth they call them because he takes a size 10 and they was 15/6 I think it is wicked price don't you and what are you going to do when you want them then you must buy but the worse is over now and we must look forward for better days so long as the war is over you don't seem to mind dear, I do hope it will not be home [?long] before you are home with us as you must [k]now it get very lonely dear only Tommy and myself dear So I hope the next mail I have will say you are coming home dear hear [here] I close with lots of love and kisses I remain your loving wife Lizzie

74 Ossory Rd
Old Kent Rd

Jan 18 [1919]

Dearest
Just a line hoping to find you in the best of health as it
leaves us both at present Well dear I have seen Edie and
she tell me old George is going on alright he is in Egypt
so that is alright Harry Evans is not home yet, I wonder
when you are coming home I don't care how soon I can
tell you as it is very lonely and it don't seem as if you are
coming home dear, or else I have lost all patience of
waiting dear I think that is what it is dear don't you
think so, Well dear I am looking forward to seeing you
this year it will be nice to have our little times together
again Little Tommy is looking forward for your coming
home dear I can tell you, he tell me he want you to come
home so as you can take the chairs and tables out and
put them in a cart like Mr Braggs did, he think it is
grand to move I can tell you all he know is he is going to
help so the quicker you come home the better it will
please him, I cannot help smiling at him he is a [k]nock-
out I can tell you, he tell me that the airplane is going to
fetch you home and drop you in the passage all I hope
you bo[u]nce as I afriad [afraid] you will get slightly
brosed [bruised] he is telling everybody about it and
that you are going to buy him a little sister never mind
he his [is] getting a fine boy dear and you will be
surprised to see him I know Well dear I now close
hoping you are quite well

I remain your loving wife Lizzie

[Written on a pre-printed paper with a floral decoration in purple and green surrounding 'A FOND WISH' and the following verse:

An old and kindly wish I send you
That all good for aye attend you
Each cloud be lined with gleaming gold
Each joy for you be manifold.]

74 Ossory Rd
Old Kent Rd
SE London

Jan 26 Sunday [1919]

Dearest
Just a line hoping you are in the pink of health as it
leaves us both at present Well dear I have been thinking
of you very much this last week, well you [k]now I am
always thinking of you dear but this week I wake up in
the night and wonder about you dear, Well the truth is I
miss you very much and I suppose that is the reason
dear I feel very loving towards you today and feel as if I
would do any think to be with you dear, it is quite a
miserable feeling dear but I cannot help it I do hope it
wont be long before you are home dear I have sent those
papers you ask for and you should get them about the
same time as this letter dear I do hope they will get you
home dear as I do want you home with us dear, I am
glad you had a nice Christmas, our's was as well as could
be expected dear the stuff being so dear we could not
have what we should have liked but you was contented,
had to be, Well dear I read in the paper that there is only
20,000 coming from the east this year, and they are to be
home not later than October the rest have got to stop till
next spring dear I do hope you will be one of those to
come this year, do your best to get home dear, write to
Mr Beber and see if you can do any good that way dear, I
am glad to hear you are still a teatoetaller [teetotaller]
for it must be alful [awful] to see those fellow[s] drunk
and not able to know what they are doing, well dear the
weather is very trying rain day after day it give on the
sick [? makes one sick] it is raining today quite a misable
[miserable] day I can tell you, with regards to the old

lady I have not been down there for over 2 years and I
see very little of the girls, young Arthur is still in
England up till Christmas and I have not seen him since,
I have very few visitors come I suppose they will all
come round I suppose thinking they will get a good
nights enjoyment Well dear you say you have sent a
parcel and I should have received it by now, as your
letter was written on Christmas day well I have not got
the parcel you speak of I received the 10£ but no parcel
dear I will write and let you [k]now as soon as I get it
dear, little Tommy is wondering when you are sending
his pocket money he said that he will tick you off for it,
someone told me the other day that they were going to
fetch the men home by airplane so Tommy said that they
would fetch you home and drop you in the passage I
could not help laughing over it, he was quite concerned
over it dear, Well dear I got two letters from you this
week, I think, somehow you will get home dear, if only
you had been in hospital when the armstrain
[?armistice] was signed and you would have got a better
change [?chance] dear but we must trust in god and he
know's best dear Well dear I must close as it is dark and
misable [miserable] afternoon I remain your loving wife

Lizzie

FRAGMENT in Lizzie's hand
Undated [?1919]
Pages 5 and 6 of a longer letter

…pay him better to stop there altogether, I said I know I
have been silly at keeping the place together as I have but
there was no reason for me to have to suffer the lonely
life because I have done my duty at home and kept
everything alright, I was more than hurt at being told
that you were alright out there I can tell you Well dear I
must now close with the best of love hoping you will not
be long before you are home I remain your loving wife

Lizzie

[incomplete] [early 1919]

...wives that should be up in arms about it, we cannot get cheaper food or clothes, but we have the smallest money of the lot, and have to give up our husband, until the government think proper to discharge them, who do you think are the worst off, I guess if they were giving a suit of karkie [khaki] they would go back to there job for ten shillings a week sooner than join up Well dear I don't care what happens so long as you get home dear, I expect you will be alright with Singers dear, as I know you were liked up there Mrs Thompson and I get on very well I think she is [a] very nice young woman, she takes a lot of notice of Tommy and let him turn her machine so you can guess he is a 1 with her, he walk in the shop, straight to Mrs Thompson and said can I turn the machine round, quite a [?common] thing every week for him Well dear I must close hoping to see you soon

I remain your loving wife

[Partly written in pencil on decorated paper with a blue/green floral edging – a title 'Remember Me' and a text in red 'Fond memories are golden links which bind glad hearts together']

74 Ossory Rd
Old Kent Rd

Feb 2 [1919]

Dear Old Tom
Just a line in answer to your letter, I received 4 letters and a parcel which has got all brass things in dear that are beautiful I like them very much, they have got here in good condition the 1lb of sugar as well better than the other parcel dear nothing broke at all, and I am very pleased with them dear, I say dear I should like some more of that brass I think they look very nice dear, I only want a nice sideboard now and then we will be landed dear. Well dear time is going on today is the second of Feb so if you are coming home in March you will have to look sharp, I am very pleased with your letters as they seem to be very cheerful and something to look forward for dear, I am putting my address on the letters at the back, in case you come home before you get these and then they will come back to us dear, well dear in regards to Bill Tyson and the crowd I should not trouble to go round there as they are not worth troubling over, I don't care a bit about them in the least, and they are jealous, they are just the same to Flo don't speak over the kids. I suppose you are getting quite excited about coming home dear well at least we are at home dear little Tommy keeps on saying you are coming home soon dear and you will have to watch your pen as he does them all in. I have had to finish this letter dear with a pencil as I cannot buy a pen because the shops are shut at 8o/c

dear. Well dear you tell me to get fit I hope you have not got much in store for me as I don't fancy my luck I can tell you old dear well never mind do not take to[o] many libity [liberties] with me, Well I wont mind so long as I have you home with me I suppose you know Mr Ward is home never been further than Sco[t]land is home doing his round old George is not home yet I have not seen anything of Kate or Grace since before the week before Christmas so I don't [k]now if Harry Evans is home dear, all I hope it will not be long before you come home as I am so longing to see you dear as you say you cannot understand me wanted you home women are very funny to take a fancy to funny things and I suppose that what has happened to me dear, I don't [k]no[w] why Tom wants you at home for I expect you will smile he is getting a lad I can tell you we are having snow hear [here], been snowing for a week, so old Tom [h]as watch his opportunity and as soon as he got out in the street he has throw a snowball at me, I have had to get cross with him he has give it to me I can tell you and killed himself laughing Well dear you will have a very good time with him when you come home I can tell you, hear [here] I close with fond love and kisses I remain your loving wife Lizzie

74 Ossory Rd
Old Kent Rd

Feb 9th Sunday [1919]

Dearest
Just a line hoping you are alright as it leaves us at home,
well dear I am looking forward to seeing you soon dear, I
have sent those papers on to you dear and by the time
you get this letter you ought to have got them Well dear
Mr Bever [Beber] told me he had sent to the head office,
and they sent a letter back saying they were sending in as
soon as the government allow them to send for there
men so if I were you I should not leave it to them I
should do all you can to get home dear there is no end of
men home some of them have not been across at all dear
and they have got there tickets, I have been told that
weather [whether] you are A1 or B2 they are keeping for
the army so you being B3 I should think you are stand a
better chance of coming home, I do hope you are home
soon dear it will be so nice wont it dear, I say there is
such a lot of trouble hear [here] with the strikers the
tubes are out, the railways and the electrical engineers
are all out I tell you things are jolly bad hear [here] the
people are going to and fro the city in a motor lorry
come right along the Kent Road, thing are very grave at
home, that is why I want you to come home as soon as
you can come dear so I think the work will be very hard
for one and all, as the labour is in awful state hear [here],
the Post Office are going to strike, they want shorter
hours abolition of split attendance and great reduction
of night hours so I don't [k]now what to think of things
some of them don't want work what I can see of it dear,
well dear I have got one parcel which had all the brass
things I like them very much dear but I have not

received the other one yet dear with silk in yet I suppose that will be longer coming dear I got the 1lb of sugar which come very useful dear, Tom wanted to ware [wear] those toe bells so I had to put them on him, I thank you for the silk, but you ought not to pay all that money dear as if is not 56 yds wide dear it will not be enough for a dress but anyway it will make me a nice blouse dear but there if I see it I will be able to see if there is enough dear it is very kind of you to think of me so but it is such a lot of money to spend on me dear. I expect you will see a difference in young Tommy he is all a boy, I leave him now with Mrs Drummond opposite and I tell you he is a lad there are two children over there one a boy about 12 the girl is 10 so you bet he is well away, My work is very quite [quiet] at present dear but I think it is all to do with the strikes and unrest at home hear [here], I don't know if young Arthur is out of the army yet dear I don't think he his [is], and do not seek[see] very much of them at home, but I don't think Harry Evans is home or he would have been down to see me, I don't think he is a bad chap the army has took a lot of swank out of him dear

Well dear I must close hoping to see you soon I remain your loving wife

Lizzie

74 Ossory Rd
Old Kent Rd

Feb 11th [1919]

Dearest
Just a line hoping you are in the best of health as it leaves
us both at present. Well dear Arthur came round to see
me he is up on a 6 days final leave he is going to
Germany, because he will not sign on for 7 years in the
colours and 5 years in the reserves will be going there
next Thursday 48 of them are picked out because they
wont sign, I do hope they will not do the same with you
dear as I am looking forward for your being at home
with us dear, old Arthur had the biggest dispointment
[disappointment] he has ever had he said they all fell in
and march to Whitehall for their discharges and when
they got there they picked out 3 of them and Arthur was
one of the three the others got there discharge paper and
these three were sent back a damn shame don't you
think so, I hope they don't work it on you like that I can
tell you, Tommy is greatly concerned about you being
black he keeps on asking if you are going black or what
makes you go black of course he has a comic every week
and I have to read it to him so there was something in
last week comic about a black me [man] going in for
some boot polish the man in the shop ask him if he
wanted black or brown the black man said black, this
tickled Tom and he thinks when you come home you
will used black polish on your face, every morning he
ask why you are going black for, is it the Indian that are
burning you black, then when I tell him it's the sun he
wants to [k]now why the sun turns you black and he can
see the joke when he thinks of your using black boot
polish on your face, well dear do you think you will be

home soon dear I am looking forward for you, Harry
Evans is not home yet dear, he is in hospital in France,
the Doctor don't seem to [k]now what is the matter with
him, he ask if he could be sent to England and the
doctor said, lay down you are not strong enough to sit
up so he must be in a nice state, well dear Tom said you
will have to scrub your face to get it clean, I tell you he is
very concerned about your face, saying nothing about
anything else, well dear I got the photo I think you look
about as happy as I do so we can shake hands, I think
there is only about me and 2 more woman in the street
that have not got their husbands home all the others
have got there home discharge and right out of it, Mrs
Wrights husband is in Egypt, the young woman across
the road husband is at Malta and you are in India, they
seem to forget the soldiers in the east altogether what I
can see of it dear, and all those chaps have only joined
up lately I don't think its fair do you Mr Ward is home
and has never been out of England and what with the
strikes and one thing another I am just about sick of it I
think they could hurry themselves a bit quicker don't
you think so, if they wanted to send a lot of troops to
France they would get them ready in about quarter of an
hour but it don't suit them to hurry for the men in the
east Mr Barrett is home he had to go at the finish and is
the first home I cannot understand it they seemed to be
getting there tickets in France and the chaps that are at
home not a word about the fellows in the east so much
red tape about the army a[h] well we must look forward
to better days dear that is all hear [here] I close hoping
you will be home soon I remain your loving wife

Lizzie

74 Ossory Rd
Old Kent Rd

[undated] [early 1919]

Dearest
Just a line hoping you are quite well dear, well I have
been all over the place and cannot do anything as the
business has not been carry on why [while] the war has
been on dear well I have seen Kate and Grace dear,
young Bert has joined up for 12 years you can bet it has
upset mother. Arthur is in Germany lying in hospital he
is very ill but we don't know what is the matter dear, I
have not seen your Carrie dear but I did hear she has got
to go right away because she is very ill it is home affairs
and the doctor said she will not be any better unless Well
dear I don't [k]now what to say only I should be glad if
you were coming home dear, my work is very quite
[quiet] at present dear well dear I will close with fond
love and kisses I remain

Your loving wife
Lizzie

74 Ossory Rd
Old Kent Rd

[undated] [from context February 1919]

Dearest,
Just a line hoping you are going on alright dear Well
dear I received parcel with silk inside dear. I think it is
very nice If it wears as well as it looks I shall be more
than pleased with it dear, well, dear, it is very kind of you
sending these nice things home but I should think more
of them if you were coming home. I don't want presents
I want you dear, nothing else matters dear, so long as you
were home dear I should be quite satisfied dear, I don't
want for money of anything else but I don't feel satisfied
enough. I am pinning [pining] for you and cannot help
it dear, in fact I am getting bitter towards the men how
[who] are at home, and cannot help it dear so the sooner
you get home the better for me dear Well dear I had a
letter from Arthur dear, he is in hospital in Germany
suffering from his kidneys again, very bad by all
accounts. Harry Evans is expecting to come home any
day dear for good, and Jhon [John] has been
discharge[d] from the army, I do hope and trust you are
the next one home for I am fed up I can tell you with
everything and anybody so you can just guess how I feel
dear, well dear hear [here] I close hoping you are soon
home I remain

Your loving wife Lizzie

74 Ossory Rd
Old Kent Rd

16 Feb [1919]

Dearest
Just a line to let you know I received parcel yesterday
Monday, with jersey and silk for which I thank you very
much dear I think the silk is very nice dear, but I shall
not have enough for a dress as it is only single [?width]
Well dear I like it very much but it seem a lot of money
to pay for it and it should be very good for the price dear
Well dear I don't think you had better buy any more as 7
yds cost 27/6 and I want another 7 yds £2-15 the cost
before paying for the making and the extras for it, I
think it will come very dear don't you think so, don't
think I am not pleased with it, because I am only it is so
much to pay I think don't you dear Well dear have you
got any idea of coming home I have not heard anything
of Singer or Mr Bever [Beber] dear, but with what I
heard I think you are getting all there men back dear, Mr
Harris and Mr Eversfield is back and started work so you
guess I am looking forward of your coming home, Well
dear the weather is alful [awful] hear [here] snow and
rain everyday I am getting fed up with the weather I can
tell you, no[t] doing the boy any good his chest is very
queer dear it is the weather dear Well I don't suppose it
will be long before dear as well I['m] looking forward for
you every day I expect you are hoping each day to be
sent home dear, Well dear Harry Evans is home he is in
hospital at Waterloo Road dear very ill he has been in
the coal mines dear and by all account be treated very
badly dear, I hear from Nell the other day and the major
wrote to her to say that Jack was killed right out dear
with a shell it is very sad and I think dear don't you the

worst that could have happened dear Well dear I have
found out when the mail goes out it is on Thursday so I
have to catch it Wednesday dear Well dear I now close
hoping you are keeping well I remain your loving wife
Lizzie

74 Ossory Rd
Old Kent Rd

Feb 20th [1919]

Dearest
Just a line hoping you are quite well as it leaves us both
at present, Well dear we have been to the pictures this
afternoon and they were very nice dear, I wonder when
you will be home to take us there dear, Well dear I have
had such a longing for you this week I cannot
understand it, I felt I would do anything to be with you I
wonder if you will be away from home much longer, I
am not depressed, but I catch myself thinking of you so
dear and dreaming all the time have to pull myself
together at times from thinking so dear, I hope you are
quite well as it is so strange for me to be like this, I
wonder if you still love as you used to dear, I do hope it
will not be long before you are home as life is not much
without you dear I can tell you Well I read in the paper
that they are getting enough troops for the army dear
Well I don't care so long as get home dear, and I expect
you feel the same, I expect you chaps are hoping to get
home dear and longing for the time to come, it seem
that all of them are at home except you I suppose it my
fancy dear, Well dear I hope you have not signed on for
longer service dear because I shall be very cross if you
have because we want to get to work as we have not got
any time to spare dear as the work hear [here] is being
snapped up, some of them are rather pleased at your not
being home, or else it my fancy dear Well dear I now
close hoping you are well

I remain your Lizzie

74 Ossory Road

Feb 24th [1919]

Dearest
Just a line hoping you are in the best of health as it leaves
us both at present, well dear I have had a lady down
from the [?] library, it has been taken over by the
Pension people she ask me when you joined up what you
were in and how much rent I paid I told her of course I
was very careful what I said to her, I ask her what it was
for, and if it was going to be stopped but she said no
only the soldiers were being discharged and of course
they were not paying any claim to them so I am waiting
for the end of the week now as we get it through every 2
months 15/- the first two months and 15/- that makes
£1-10 per qr I don't think they are going to stop it of
course I did not tell her I was at work I will let you know
if I get it through alright dear I do hope you will not be
long before you are home dear I am getting sick of this
rotten life dear, and I [k]now you must be, but there you
must be coming home as it said that all men joined in
1914 and 1915 were being discharged by March 20th and
that is only another month dear, I expect you are like me
dear don't know what to put in your letters I am so sorry
you so downhearted dear but cheer up our time is
coming and you may be home before you think dear
Well dear this is all I have to say at present

I remain your loving wife
Lizzie

74 Ossory Rd
Old Kent Rd

Feb 28 [1919]

Dearest
Just a line hoping you are quite well as it leaves us both
at present, Well dear I have been up and seen Mr Beber
and ask him if he had put a claim in for you dear he said
he had sent to the head office and he was shur [sure]
they had sent for you dear, but he would write to the
head office again and tell them I had been making
inquiries about it, he said he thought it was the distance
but he would let me know what they said by next week
dear, so I will write and let you know dear I think by all
accounts you will not be long before you are home with
us dear, and then I will be so glad, Well dear I received a
letter from the War Pensions Committee that is the
people who have taken over the S.S. [indecipherable]
asking me what I was getting allowed me I told them
£2-5 per quarter and also made all enquiries what I was
getting it for, I believe they are going to stop it I will let
you know if I hear anymore dear Well dear I have got
hope of seeing you soon so cheer up all well that ends
well hear [here] I close hoping to hear from you

I remain your loving wife Lizzie

74 Ossory Rd
Old Kent Rd

[undated] [from context March 1919]

Dearest
Just a line hoping to find you in the best of health as it
leaves us both at present dear, Well dear I am still
waiting and hoping each day that each mail will have a
letter to say that you are coming home dear, I think Mr
Beber has put in for you dear by what I heard Well dear
your brother George is coming home and Bob is going
[getting] married next Sunday, I do not go round there,
but I met the woman that lives in Pop's and she told me
about it dear, My brother George is expected home this
week, so I should not think it will be long before you are
home dear, and wont we have a good time together dear
Well dear I really do not know what to put in this letter,
little Tommy is looking forward for your coming home I
dont know what you have got to buy for him when you
get here so you had better have plenty of money or else
he will tell you off has [as] he calls it dear he his [is]
growing a fine boy every one takes notice of him dear I
was at the butcher's the other day and the lady behind
the counter said what a fine boy he is and what lovely
eyes he has got of course you bet I am very proud of
him, even when he goes up to Singer's shop they let him
turn the machine round and that pleases him to[o] Well
dear I cannot think what to say in this letter only I do
hope it will not be long before you are home, I remain
your

Loving wife Lizzie

74 Ossory Rd
Old Kent Road

March 2nd [1919]

Dearest
Just a line hoping you are keeping well as it leaves us
both at present dear Well dear I am still looking forward
to your coming home dear which I hope will not be long
dear I hear there is a ship come in last Friday to
Plymouth but I don't suppose you are on that one but
we will hope for the next one dear Well dear I still love
you a lot I often dream of you dear I do wish you were
home dear as the time is so long dear and life is so
misable [miserable] on ones own I suppose you feel
flatter when I write to you like this dear but I mean it I
am not joking even little Tommy is looking forward to
your coming home, all the children seem to have there
dads home expect [except] him and he feel it I can tell
you, I buy him a comic every week, and I have to read it
to him and there was a bit in this weeks tickled him, it
was about the soldiers getting there tickets one soldier
goes to the doctors and ask him if he could give the
officers a dose of something so as to hurry them up, for
he said be [by] the time he got his ticket he would be an
old grandfather the way he was discharging them and
young Tom killed himself a laughing at it, he is a funny
kid, Well dear you will be surprise[d] at him I can tell
you Well dear I suppose you will let me know when you
are coming home as I want to make the place look nice
and fresh dear Well dear I now close hoping to hear from
you soon

Lizzie

74 Ossory Rd
Old Kent Rd

March 4 [1919]

Dearest
Just a line hoping you are quite well as it leaves us at
present, dear well dear I don't know what we are going
to do but Mr Larham the landlord is going to put 3
shillings per week on our rent dear write back and let me
know what you think about it dear, you ask me in your
last letter if prices are going down, what I can see of it
they are going up, well dear I wrote you a letter last week
telling you about the [?] liberty I have got this month
which is 15/- dear but I [of] course I have no idea what
is going to happen within the next month dear I saw Mr
Beber dear and he told me they had put a claim in for
you so I should think you will soon be home dear, Well
dear the weather here is alful [awful] rain rain all the
week enough to give one the pip if you have not already
got it, write and let me know if you have got any idea
when you will be home dear as in your last letter you
said Christmas I hope you will be home before that old
dear, as I don't think I shall be able to hold out as long as
that so do you[r] best to get home before Christmas I
say I think we shall have to have something better for a
living as they tell me at singer it is alful [awful] they have
cut the packs up too small that it is not enough for the
girls living [?leaving] out the men of course young Kate
has pack[ed] up there, she has got a job for a firm under
clothes [?]collectoring a good job to[o] by what I can
hear of it dear something after Savage's job, you know
this job I have got is a good one I can tell you I shall be
sorry to have to pack it up dear Old Savage is one of the
best to work for I don't know what['s] the matter dear

but I keep on putting letter in this letter all wrong dear you must excuse me but I cannot help it that is what it is Well dear I am sending the cards with this letter dear you are asking for I have already sent some and you should have received them by now dear you ask me of Mr Miles I cannot tell you as they don't live here now they have been gone some time dear, but I do [k]now of a case where a man was in the flower trade you know making wreaths, they have got a shop in Great Dover St one of my customers and he has got out of it dear, Well you do you[r] best dear, I must now close I remain your's Lizzie

PS I am sending you cards memorandums and agreements so look out for them dear

Damaged fragment
[from context March1919]

Page out of order:

> …asking for you back [?] in civil life again, so Mr [?
> Beber] has sent it on to you [?] with a letter inside telling
> you [?he] has applied for you which [?you] will read is
> very nicely [?put] together and also he has [?] the letter
> and sent [?it] off while I was in the office [?you] see
> there will be no mistake at you not getting [?] dear, so
> when you get [?it] you have got to take…

Remainder of letter:

> …George is home from Egypt his firm Hardings put a
> claim in for him he has got his discharge altogether, and
> he has [?been] up to see them about his job they're
> offering him £2 standing and he wont take it dear but we
> can see to ourselves when you come home, dear all you
> want is being discharged out of the army and then we
> can start on our own dear you understand dear don't
> you, Well dear I thought I would write and tell you all
> about the letter, you must excuse me as it is Tuesday
> morning and I have got my book to do dear I shall be
> looking forward for you every day now dear hear [here]
> I close with love I remain your loving wife Lizzie

74 Ossory Rd
Old Kent Rd

March 7 [1919]

Dearest

Just a note hoping you are going quite well dear you ask
me in the last letter if Mr Miles is home of course you
[k]now they give up the shop dear when he joined up
and I have heard that he is in France dear there is new
people there now, so of course he don't come under the
one man business order dear as they sold the shop dear,
Well dear my brother George is home out of it altogether
got his ticket last Wednesday he told me that you have
got to do another year because you never joined up till
1916 for Gods sake don't stop there another year if you
can help it dear I have send head bills, cards, and papers
off to you and you ought to get them before this letter
dear, I have been looking forward for your coming dear,
but it has upset me to think you may have to do another
year dear do write and let me know if there is anything
in it dear I feel quite down hearted about it dear, I have
not received that £4 you spoke of in your last letter dear
as I got the letter last Saturday that would be March 2nd
saying that you were going to send the £4 but I have not
got it yet dear, Well I hope to have a little better news the
next letter you send weather [whether] you are coming
home or not dear Well dear I will close with best love I
remain your loving wife Lizzie

74 Ossory Rd
Old Kent Rd

March 14 [1919]

Dearest
Just a line hoping you are quite well as it leaves us both
at present well dear do you think you will be home soon
the food in prices hear [here] are dropping dear Marg is
9d and they think by the summer dear there will be a big
drop in prices dear, I expect you have got the letter from
Mr Beber dear, Well dear I received £4 yesterday what
you sent us dear I thank you dear Well dear I have not
much to say only I hope you will soon be home dear, of
course you know George is home dear and Harry Evans
is in hospital at present but he is going on alright dear,
you seem to be very downhearted in your letter which I
got last Monday but cheer up I don't think you will be
out there long dear now, and then we will be happy
together again dear Mr Harris at Singers is back with
them again Well dear you must excuse short letter as I
have not got much to say dear Will close with fond love

I remain your loving wife
Lizzie

74 Ossory Rd
Old Kent Rd

March 19th [1919]

Dearest
Just a line hoping you are in the pink of health as it
leaves us at present Well dear I hope you have got the
papers and also Mr Beber['s] letter, Well dearie I am very
sorry to hear you are so down hearted dear but cheer up
as I think there is a good time before us as I have said
before it [is] a long lane that has not a turning, I should
think there is a turning for us two dear, Well dear I don't
know what to put in this letter, only I hope you will not
be long before you are home with us dear, well dear they
said the miners were to be the first men discharged Well
dear if you were hear [here] to see the way in which we
are getting our coals it is disgraceful I should not think it
matter weather [whether] it was dustmen as the labour
is very much [?]uninterested here dear, well if you get
home dear we can arrange for something which will suit
us Well you must be fed up with being out there, I know
we are at home, wait, wait, day after day and no change
at all but never mind all well that end well so don't
worry old dear and keep your eyes open for them letters
from the firm and also cards and headbills dear I got the
4£ also one parcel with silk and Jercey [jersey] one with
brass stuff in dear, that makes two parcels and 4£ I have
got dear up to now Well dear I will close with love I
remain your loving wife

Lizzie

74 Ossory Road
Old Kent Road

March 22 [1919]

Dearest
Just a line hoping things are going well with you as it
leaves us both at present dear, Well dear I have got
something to tell you Singers have got your name up on
the roll of honour dear, Well dear do you think you will
be home soon dear I am looking forward to your
coming dear, I saw Mr Eversfield today and he told me
the firm have applied for you and you should be in
England in about 6 weeks from now the least dear Well
dear you will be surprise at the boy he has grown so and
not in the least babyfied at all, he tell me I am a silly little
Mother, that is if I don't do things as I should to suit him
dear, they say we are going to have peace in next week, so
I say roll on what do you think about it dear, Well dear I
hear you have a famine out there, are you getting your
food alright, or shall I send you some dear, I feel very
much worry about it so do write and let me know if I
could send you anything dear, we are going along nicely
here margarine is only 8d per pound now so that is
better and no Ration for it so that is better dear I think
things will be better as time goes on dear if only you
were at home dear to share it, I should be much happier
dear but there we must be patience [patient] and things
will come right in the end dear Well dear I must close
with kind love I remain your loving wife

Lizzie

74 Ossory Rd
Old Kent Road

March 24 [1919]

Dearest
Just a line I don't [k]now what to put in the letter from
time to time only I wish I had a letter from you to say
you were going to come home dear, Well dear this is
Sunday dear I am getting sick of this life dear and I
expect you feel the same, of course we expected this
when the war was on but the war is over and you ought
to be home with us, Of course dear I am grumbling at
you but you [k]now how I feel at home here waiting
patiently wondering when you will be home dear, it is
quite a[n] anxious time I can tell you, it is a sort of no
room for you anywhere because you have not got your
old man with you, but wait till you do come home dear,
there is only room for me and no one else what do you
think that Mr Barrett is home and out of it and you
[k]now when he joined dont you, well dear I am hoping
wont be long before you are home, as the time do hang
on I can tell you, of course you [k]now Harry Evans is
home he is doing well now has gone on his 2 months
leaves dear Well this is a short rotten letter but I don't
[k]now what to put in it so will close hoping the next
one will be better dear With best love and kisses

I remain you loving wife Lizzie
PS I still love you every so much dear

74 Ossory Rd
Old Kent Road

March 29 [1919]

Dearest

Just a line hoping everything is going well dear Well dear
you ought to have every hopes of coming home to us
dear I am very lonely dear, I am hoping you will not be
long before you are with us as, I expect you feel very
lonely dear and looking forward for coming home to us
dear, Well dear it seems years since I last saw you or was
with you dear little Tommy is looking forward for you
coming he wants to [k]now why all the other daddys are
home and not you dear, he think you have not killed all
the Indians dear, Well dear they say absent make the
heart grow fonder and I believe it to[o] for at time dear I
don't [k]now what to do with myself I feel so misable
[miserable] I do try and buck myself up but it is no use
dear I feel as if I have lost something dear, I wonder if
you will be long before you are with us, I do pray to God
it wont be long dear I say my prayers every night and ask
him to send you home to us dear and one cannot do
anymore dear, Well dear are you better in your health
than you were dear, I have had a bad cold but am much
better of it now dear, Well dear if only I had a letter
today you were coming home I should be pleased dear
the time waiting is a sort of hungry feeling dear, I get
very sad at times dear but I cannot help it, I do try and
make the best of it dear so you must forgive me I have
been very misable [miserable] today don't [k]now why I
suppose I miss you still near time I got used to it but I
don't think I shall ever get used to it dear do you Well
dear I must close hoping you will not be long before you
are home with us again

I remain your loving wife Lizzie

74 Ossory Rd
Old Kent Rd

March 30 [1919]

[letter has a small profile head drawn on last page]

Dearest
Just a line hoping you are quite well as it leaves both at
present dear, Well dear do you think you will be home
shortly dear, I am looking forward dear, I think those
photos are lovely dear, the only fault with them is that
you should have had your head turning round this way
facing us dear, otherwise they are very nice Well dear do
you think that you will be coming home dear I would
like to know dear I have been told that there is a lot of
troops coming home from India I do hope you will be
lucky enough to get home dear with these, little Tommy
was very pleased with his hankicheafe [handkerchief]
dear he has been very queer on the chest dear again, I get
very much afraid of him when he gets these attacks dear,
of course I think it has all to do with the house as you
know it is very damp and of course the [that] is no good
to him dear, of course I have as many fires as I can only
the coal has been very short dear and of course I have
had to go very careful with it, but when you do come we
must make difference [different] arrangements dear for
the boys sake dear every winter I have this [? threat] dear
it['s] such a nuisance to[o], well
dear you must excuse short letter it
is so late and I have been washing so
I am tired Close with kind love I
remain your loving wife Lizzie.

74 Ossory Rd
Old Kent Rd

April 6 [1919]

Dearie
Just a line hoping you are quite well as it leaves us at
present, Well dear, I have not had a letter since Feb 27th
that was the date you wrote it dear but it is 2 week ago
when I got 3 letters al[to]gether, 1reg, the other two
quite usele [usual], and I have been in the habit of
getting a letter a week is there any thing wrong dear, I
feel a little bit worried about it dear I do hope you are
alright dear Well dear do you think you will be coming
home dear I do hope it will not be long now dear, little
Tommy is getting quite a big boy now he has gone to
Sunday school today dear and quite please over it dear,
you will be surprise at him dear when you see him no
baby ways at all, as big as the other children of 12 years
old in his way dear, I see Mr Beber last week and he told
me he had put in a claim for you and you should be
getting on the way home by now if not hear [here], Well
dear Harry Evans has had a month of his leave, they gave
him 2 he think he will get his discharge because his heart
is out of it[s] place of course he is going before a board
when he goes back, Well dear take care of yourself I must
now close hoping you will soon be home dear

I remain your wife
Lizzie

74 Ossory Rd
Old Kent Rd

April 8 [1919]

Dearest
Just a line in answer to your letter which I received dear I
will do my best with that letter dear I am going about it
this afternoon dear and I will let you know how I get on
I have had to have a lot of running about dear as it has
been rather a trouble to[o] but I think I shall be on the
right scent this afternoon dear, well dear you ought to
have had that letter from Mr Beber by now and that
alone ought to do all that is needed dear but I will do my
best to[o] Well dear I am very much dispointed
[disappointed] about it I think it is a shame don't you
dear I received necklace and I think it is very very pretty
dear, well dear I have made inquiries about it and they
tell me that, you must wait dear as Singers have put in
for you dear they cannot do anything in the matter dear
Well dear trust to luck dear I think it will be alright dear
Well dear I will now close hoping you are quite well I
remain your loving wife Lizzie

Excuse short writing as I want to catch the post. I remain
your loving wife
Lizzie

74 Ossory Road
Old Kent Rd

April 13th [1919]

Dearest
Just a line hoping you are going on alright dear, I have
not had a letter from you dear this week I hope nothing
is wrong with you dear I suppose you don't know if you
will coming home dear it is a long wait dear, and only
those that are place[d] in the same way can feel for one
little Tommy is hoping it wont be long before you come
home with us dear, I think the world is very unfair the
way things are done, it seem to me those that have had a
good time why [while] the war was on are still having a
good time dear so have never been away from home
other[s] have had to do there share dear I cant
understand why they don't make those men join and
release the lakes [likes] of you as I thing [think] 3 years
service is quite long enough to give [?] gratis and that is
what you have done 3 years next month the 7th dear I
know only to[o] well I can tell you as it has been no life
for me at home, what with the putting up with high
prices and low money as I have been taken dear has been
a real trial I can tell you dear, well dear it['s] no us[e]
grumbling I suppose but it makes one get fed up I can
tell you dear, and I expect you are just the same dear, but
you ought to have got the letter from singers by now
dear and that ought to do what is needed dear all I hope
is that you will be home with us soon dear hear [here] I
close with the best of luck

I remain your loving wife Lizzie Love from little Tommy

74 Ossory Rd
Old Kent Rd

April 16th [1919]

Dearest
Just a line in answer to your letter which I received this
morning well dear I am pleased that you are getting my
letter dear, as you must look forward to them dear, the
weather has changed a great deal here but I am no lover
of the hot weather to[o] trying walking about in it dear,
I like Tommy shoes very much he has worn them to[o]
they look very nice dear, you ask me if I have change[d],
I don't think I have dear, I think I should like to go out
of London for a while dear, and I think it will be a wise
thing to go into business, as the work is very quite
[quiet] here, Well dear you say I promised you
something when you come home, I suppose you will
catch me in silly modes [moods], like you did when I
drop in for Tommy still I have not much to grumble at I
suppose, little Tom is 5 years old but not all your fault
dear, it['s] because you have been done out of your
luxury for a long time, I will get the book, I have ordered
it for you and I will send it to you dear, Well I must close
as Tommy is wanting to go to bed, I remain your loving
wife

Lizzie

74 Ossory Rd
Old Kent Rd

April 17 [1919]

Dearest
Just a line hoping you are quite well as it leaves us both
at present dear, well dear I received a letter from you this
morning dear I have got £4 what you sent dear I have
also got the parcel which had the brass dear, you ought
to have got that letter from Singers by now dear. It has
come from St Pauls Churchyard the head office dear, I
think it will do all that should be done dear, I have not
met with much luck at the advisory committee dear but
cannot tell you all at present dear, they have promised to
do there best for me and they will let me know dear, Well
dear tomorrow is Good Friday another holiday and you
not at home to share it with us dear, of course our
George is dismobed [demobbed] on 5 years reserved
dear Well dear I wish you was home I am beginning to
get tired and sick of this life dear, you know I sort of feel
weary of this wait wait wait dear Harry Evans is going on
alright know [now], of course he is not well by a long
way but he is going on very well, he took Tommy out for
the day last Sunday and Tom enjoyed hiself very much
he like Tommy and Tom like him I can tell you, little
Tom is very interesting now to everyone, you will be
surprise at him when you do come home dear I never
got a letter last Saturday so I said to Tom no letter from
Dad again, he said never mind perhaps he is coming
home and he cannot write to us Mum they don't write
when theyre coming home I had to laugh myself dear

Well must close hoping to have good news Lizzie

74 Ossory Rd
Old Kent Rd

April 27 [1919]

Dearest
Just a line hoping you are in the best of health as it leaves
us both at present Well dear I wonder if you will be
home soon I should think you ought to and you should
have got that letter from Singers I have been hoping I
should have had a letter saying you got it and was please
for it dear, Well dear it is snowing very much dear today
and also very cold it is a blizzard I should think the
weather has been very much unsettled this last few week
one day the sun shining next day snowing or pouring of
rain, Well dear you have been a soldier for 3 years come
the 7th May and that will be some time next week dear I
am getting so sick of this sort of life dear and I expect
you feel the same towards it, I do hope you will be home
soon dear, I do hope you will not be kept dear do you
think they will dear I have done my best with that letter
you sent but have got to wait dear as they cannot do
anythink at present Well dear I must close hoping to get
some good news the next time you write I remain your
loving wife Lizzie

74 Ossory Rd
Old Kent Rd

[undated] [May 1919]

Dearest
Just a line to let you know we are going on alright Well
dear I think you ought to be home before Christmas by
the way things are in the paper dear, Well dear time is
getting on now you are getting well into four year[s] of
serving for the army dear, I am tired of writing dear, I do
hope you are quite well dear, little Tommy starts at
school next Tuesday dear, I am shur [sure] [you] will be
surprised at him when you see him, he is getting a
cheeky little monkey I can tell you, with regards to
things in England, it is in a[n] alful [awful] state I can
tell you dear there are hundred[s] of men out of work, it
make[s] one wonder what is going to happen next dear,
everybody is worried what I can see of it, there 7000
men to be discharged at the arsenal this week, unsettled
men at home is alful [awful] everything is up side down
with what I can see of things, well dear this is all at
present hear [here] I close hoping it will not be too long
before you are home again

I remain your loving wife Lizzie

74 Ossory Road
Old Kent Road

May 26th [1919]

Dearest
Just a line hoping you are alright dear I received your
letter dear saying you did not think you would be home
before the autumn well dear I am very sorry as I did
think you get home before that time dear, little Tommy
starts school next week he wants to go badly too, but I
should have sent him to school before only I am rather
afraid of the road the Old Kent Road as there has been a
lot of children knock down in that road, of late, dear,
Well dear you have ask me lots of times about going into
business Well the idear [idea] is quite alright I shall do as
you think best dear Harry Evans has gone back, so I
don't know what they will do with him Arthur is in
hospital in Germany very ill and Bert has been and
joined up for 12 years the young fool. Old John has been
put on the army of occupation and has been told off for
India he is very much upset Well dear I cannot seem to
write at all tonight I am getting very slack at writing and
as for spelling dear I am getting very bad I[k]now I have
made a mistake as soon as I have written the word no
do[ubt] you can see what I mean dear, it is so miserable I
think it is to do with the air raids I got run down dear,
everybody seem to be like that dear, well dear I hope it
has not been to[o] bad in India as by what I see in the
paper you have been fighting out there dear, as you see I
have bought a book dear I think they are very
comfortable to write on dear, there is a rare lot of men
down the street out of the army dear the lady next door
expect her husband home any day dear, so I don't think
there is many more to come now dear, Well dear I must
close hoping to hear from you soon dear I am your
loving wife Lizzie

74 Ossory Rd
Old Kent Rd

June 4th [1919]

[incomplete]

Dearest

Received your letter saying you were coming home dear
I do hope it is true dear perhaps dear you will get better
in time if you were home I am very sorry to hear you are
ill and in hospital again, I am certain India don't suit you
dear by the way you have gone out there I think myself
you ought not to have been kept in the army after you
were so bad at Tonbridge dear it is a shame dear I am so
sorry for you, Well dear little Tommy has started school
dear, he is getting on alright to[o] he is wanting you to
come home dear I have taking him to Rolls Road school
dear this week rather strange to him at first but I think
he will get on alright dear, it is quite pretty to see the
children there and how they teach them, dear Well dear I
have seen kate and Grace they are getting on very well
dear with regards to your [indistinct] it is not so bad,
but I like your cheak [cheek] practising on me, you have
got a [indistinct]...

74 Ossory Road
Old Kent Road

June 28th [1919]

Dearest
Just a line hoping you are quite better Well dear do you
think are coming home dear I think myself dear they
ought to send you home dear as you do no[t] seem to be
at all well since you have been out there of course Bill
Pascoe is home for good dear well dear I am sending the
boy to school dear, he is getting on very well to[o] he
likes it dear, I have to take him and bring him home as it
is very risky across the Kent Rd, I am sending him to
Rolls Road, that is the school I first started at many years
ago dear, well dear the[y] are expecting the peace to be
signed this week dear everybody think we shall have
peace I hope we do dear well dear this is a very short
letter but really I don't know what to put in it dear you
ask me what I meant by George being put on the
reserved, well what I can make of it dear he is ready to be
called up within 5 years if wanted dear Well dear I now
close I am so sick of writing to you I want you at home
and I shall be quite satisfied dear I remain your loving
wife Lizzie

74 Ossory Road
Old Kent Road

July 3rd [1919]

Dearest
Just a few lines hoping you are better than you were
when you last wrote, well dear we have got peace at last
just think after all this time dear everybody seems
pleased about it dear, well dear it is near time just on five
years of war Tommy has been having a good time at
school dear sports and tea parties all week and half
holidays as well he likes going to school dear I cannot get
him to stop away at all I am very pleased I can tell you
well dear I don't know for the life of me what to put in
this letter I am getting tired of writing to you I want to
see you and speak to you dear and is rotten to keep on
saying things with paper and pen dear I want see you
and I know you feel the same dear well they tell me that
there is a lot of troops coming home from India I
wonder if you could be with them I do hope so dear no
one knows how I want you home I am getting so
discontented with everyone and everything dear I don't
like this house I don't like the people about in fact I
don't like myself I am fed up with all of it dear so I do
hope for my own sake dear, well dear I hope it will not
be long before you are home I remain your loving wife
Lizzie

74 Ossory Rd
Old Kent Rd

July 6th [1919]

Dearest
Just a line in answer to your letter which I received last
Saturday, well dear when [do] you think you are coming
home dear I do hope it will not be long dear as I am very
lonley [lonely] dear, I am getting depressed very much
lately, I am seeing first one and then the other home that
I am wonding [wondering] what I have done it seems
never ending time dear I do wish you were home, the
boy is not well at all I have given him a dose of medicine
and put him to bed but he is very queer dear, Well dear
they have got the peace terms through dear I am very
glad to[o] I can tell you dear I think you will be home
soon now I cant see why the[y] want to keep you dear

Well dear this is all I have got to say I remain your loving
wife Lizzie

74 Ossory Road
Old Kent Road
July 9th [1919]

[incomplete]

Dear
Just a line in answer to your letters which I received this
morning, with regards to answering your one half of the
things you ask me, I cannot understand if it is the bank
you are referring to there is £170 in it , I don't think
there is much I fail to tell you, with regards to the books,
I had to order them and then the agent could not get
them for a month, I got two and then you wrote and
told me not to send them, I can tell you, I am just about
fed up with this sort of life, it is not at all honey as you
think it is being at home here, I have got little Tommy ill
in bed with a very bad throat the doctor coming in every
day and that is 2/ per day dear, what with the prices
being so high and also being mother and father and the
breadwinner as well I think I have got quite enough at
present to put up with this end, don't [k]now what you
think about it…

74 Ossory Road
Old Kent Road

July 12 [1919]

Dearest
Just a line to let you little Tommy is much better the
doctor said I am to keep him very quite [quiet], Well
dear I am getting lately that I cannot put up with much
more of this life you [k]now that things are very dear
here and that makes it worse as you cannot afford to be
ill now, little Tommy has got up for the first time today
dear he look very queer to[o] and I can tell you, I am
very much worried about him, now the peace is signed
and everything is alright I do not see why they want to
keep you dear Well dear I do hope they will soon send
you home Well dear I now close

Hoping you will be home soon your loving wife Lizzie

74 Ossory Road
Old Kent Road

July 27th [1919]

Dearest
Received letter from you yesterday dear I am very much
disappointed at you not coming home, don't you think
you will be home this year they don't seem to trouble
about you chaps out there why is it, well dear, I am very
much upset over your not coming home all the others
are getting home first I don't think there is any more to
come home in this street of course we have been
married 6 years come 3 days time and you still away I
am getting fed up I can tell you if there is not some
change for me soon, I am afraid I shall not be able to put
up with it dear much longer, I know if you had been at
home and waited for your calling up papers you would
have been discharged by now dear well never mind

Will close with kind regards

I remain your loving wife Lizzie

74 Ossory Rd
Old Kent Road

[undated – from context August 1919]
[incomplete]

Dearest
Just a line hoping you are going on alright dear Well
dear I received 7£ the 12£ and 15£ alright dear I have put
it away alright, Well dear when do you think you are
coming home I have been wondering if you have signed
on for longer service as it is very funny at you not being
home by now, I am getting disatisfied seeing every one
happy and I have got to struggle on day after day with
myself dear, I told you when you first joined up there
was plenty to go before you, you see we are no better off
at your joining up when you did or joining up when Mr
Barrett did he is the best off, home again and back to
work been home some month now dear. Well dear it is
very kind of you to write such nice letter but every time I
get a letter from you I feel as if I am being treating
unfair, and you don't seem to be coming home any the
quicker than when the war was on, I suppose I have got
to put up with it Well dear your sister Carrie in the street
she spoke to me and ask me if you were home I told her
now [no] I felt I could not be servel [civil] to her I felt so
damn wild she said you are better off being out were
[where] you are than being at home here, I said yes he
would be if he had not got a good home and a good wife
he would…

74 Ossory Road
Old Kent Road

Aug 19th [1919]

Dearest
Just a line hoping to find you in the best of health as it
leaves us both at present, Well dear when do you think
you are coming home dear, do you know it is over two
years since we were together dear I am thinking it is near
time you were home with us, Well dear it is very hot hear
[here] and you [k]now I don't like the summer dear I
always get very relaxed Well dear by the way things are
looking what with strikes and high prices it is as much as
one can put up with Well dear little Tommy is such a
dear kid I don't think you will get much room to make
love to me, for he is as jelous [jealous] of George or
Arthur kissing me and wont let them do it I can tell you
he said to me, I do love you mum and holds me as tight
as he can dear Well dear this is such a rotten pen and the
shops are shut or I would buy another one dear Hear
[Here] I close with love and kisses

I remain your loving wife Lizzie

74 Ossory Road
Old Kent Road

August 21st [1919]

Dearest
Just a line hoping you are quite well as it leaves us both
at present, Well dear don't you think you will home
before Christmas dear, it do seem such a long time dear
by what I read in the paper dear, I see they are going to
bring all the troops away dear, from India so I hope you
are one of the lucky ones dear that will be with those
book for home dear, I am getting tired of waiting dear, it
seem ages since I saw you and I expect you feel the same
dear but never mind all comes right in the end, you
[k]now Tommy was 5 years old last May and when you
joined the army dear he was only 1 year and 10 month, it
is a weary wait dear don't you think so, well dear the
weather is much colder now that it has been I don't
mind this sort of weather it is much better, Well dearie I
received the 7£ 12£ 15£ so you need not worry about
that dear well I expect you are looking forward at for
coming home as much as we are looking forward to
seeing you dear Well dear this is all I have to say at
present I remain

Your loving wife
Lizzie

Note: This is the last letter from Lizzie in the recovered
correspondence

Letters from Tom

ॐ

ONLY TWO LETTERS FROM TOM TO Lizzie were found. The first, dated 20 April 1919 confirms his address in India and also his rank, regiment and service number. It also illustrates the dating and postal problems involved in their dialogue by post. He refers in the text to receiving three letters from Lizzie in the mail that week. From the context they appear to be letters sent by her in March and certainly her letter dated 30 March (from the context).

The second letter, undated and incomplete, appears to have been written to signal the end of his time in India and his return home in the autumn of 1919. It is quite different in tone from any of the letters and suggests that Tom was a thoughtful man who was considering the implications of their reunion after more than two years.

245307
Gunner TJ Green
1097 Battery RFA
Mhow
India
Sunday 20/April/1919

[incomplete]

Dearest
Another mail Dear from you this week I have got three
letters with this mail Dear. The more the merrier I say I
don't mind how many I get let em all come There is no
doubt that you hardly know what to say but say anything
Dear as long as you write a letter You don't want to get
downhearted about me being away Dear as things are as
they are and if you worry yourself Dear you will not do
any good but do yourself harm by fretting. I know Dear
it must be very hard for you to see men like Barrett who
have hung back to the last minute get home before me
but we are temporarily unlucky and we must put up
with it with the best grace possible Dear. After all
Darling it will not be so over long before I am home as I
expect to be home before Christmas and that is not so
far off is it Dear. It is a damned shame but we are
powerless to do anything else other than put up with it
which we must do for the sake of ourselves Don't think
that I feel inclined to submit to such injustice quietly
only I realise it is the best to do so. I am glad to hear that
Baby is making such a fine boy Dear Bye [By] the way
what school do you send him to. I am longing to see him
Dear he must be altered to when I last saw him. I daresay
he was delighted with his shoes Dear when he saw them
I can just imagine his face when you too[k] them out of

the parcel. I daresay he is all eagerness when you are opening a parcel I am very glad the shoes fit him Dear they are nice ones as for your shoes Darling I am sorry they don't fit you Dear I was half afraid they would not do as I thought they were not broad enough they were the only pair of that shape I could get Dear. You must sell them Dear and get yourself a pair with the money. I am glad you like the brass Dear I have got some more of it which I will be sending home soon Dear. How do you like that throne thing I am glad Tommy got his handkerchiefs Dear and his 2/- I am afraid he will have to wait a while for more as I cannot get P.O's out here only very seldom I am glad you like the Photos Dear I noticed they were taken side faced myself but I never noticed when they were being done as I was getting my horse to stand right. I sent another lot of them in an ordinary envelope some which I printed from negatives myself have you got those yet. Have you received my letter asking you to send me the Motor Cycle out each week Dear You say Mr Eversfield said the firm have made application for me Dear I know that Dear that is the slip I got from Beber last week I have given the slip in to the Office and they have placed me on the list of slip men.

[His last latter from India – 1919]
[incomplete]

Well darling I don't know what you think about it dear but at last we are to get together after over two years. This is not so much as some others have had to put up with dear as they will have been away from their homes 4 or 5 years. I daresay I will have altered a great deal darling in ways appearance and manner of thought but I don't think my ordinary nature has altered much dear. But I hope all changes in me (and they will show very clear in you[r] sharp eyes) will be for the better. I think they are dear, and changes in yourself dear will they be for the better if they are I am lucky and shall glorify in them but if they are for the worse I shall shut my eyes to them and remember that you are a darling and much better than myself in any case. For your bad points to me dear are only surface and superficial but your goodnesses are deep and everlasting, loyal and strong faithful and loving – that is quite good enough in one woman; a perfect thing is insipid dear. There will be times in the future dear when we shall have to stick together work together and sacrifice together as things are not going to be too good in England and unless we do these things dear we shall experience hard times and bad times. But if we go on in our old way each one working for the other we shall be happy dear. We have had some troubled times dear this last four years and after Christmas please God our future happiness will rest largely in our own hands darling and we must make the most of it.

Well how is little Tommy getting along dear I am sorry I have not been able to get him a present but I shall get him one when I come home dear. I suppose you told him I am coming home and I daresay he is wondering in his mind what sort of man I am. I'll guarantee I am something great in his mind there is no doubt that I have a great reputation to live up to as regards Tommy. Must see what I can do for him perhaps he thinks of me as a kind of safer-cowboy perhaps he will be right. I can run and jump and ride in a way I never thought I would and no doubt it will satisfy him if I jump over a chair now and again and balance you and him on the end of my little finger. I will do my best to please him dear.

I have not made up my mind with regard to Singers dear they are waiting for me to get back I know but I suppose my experience will be something similar to George's – they will offer me an absurd salary for these days and if they do darling I shall take it but only for as long as it will take you and I to get settled in business. I shall be fetching enough money home with me dear for us to have a jolly good time during the months furlough. And then start work right away in the new year. I hope you got that big thick overcoat dear I bought just before I joined up dear I shall want that.

Well I close my last letter from India here darling, I hope to be with you in nine or ten days after you get this letter.

So goodbye for a little while darling

From your loving old mate

Tom

1941

❦

ONE LETTER FROM LIZZIE TO TOMMY – now called Tom – survives from the Second World War. Her style and spelling remain familiar.

95 Burbage Rd
Dulwich Village
SE24

Tuseday 23
1941

Dear Tom
Just a line in answer to your letter I am glad you got cig
and choclate alright, So you have got your LAC. I am
glad about it, you will get rich quick now, about your
getting home Friday who [why] don't you try and get to
Hearn[Herne] Hill station it will not be so far for you in
the blackout to walk it will get dark now soon about
quarter to eight, and very dark to[o]. Well Tom I will tell
you about Bingo when you come home on Friday, he did
not suffer at all and we was with him to the last. It seem
very funny at home without him I can tell you, Eileen
was cut up about it to[o], Well Tom I do not think there
is much more to say. By the way Annie's husband had
died and was bury [buried] last Friday week, but he has
been ill for 2 years now poor old Pat is still away he
[k]now about it to[o], well Tom I must close now

with Kind Regards I remain yours Mum Dad and Eileen

Afterword

IN THE RETRIEVED FAMILY PAPERS THERE are bundles of legal correspondence relating to the later lives of the family, but almost no personal letters. Nevertheless I have been able to piece together an outline of what happened to Lizzie's family.

The reader of Lizzie's letters may have noted that in 1919 she mentions her dream of moving house, perhaps away from London. She refers to Tom's interest in going into business, as well as the possibility of having another child, especially a girl.

These things were achieved. Their daughter, Eileen Elizabeth Green, was born in August 1923. By that time their address was in the Old Kent Road.

At some point between the wars Tom established a furniture dealing business of which one photograph and some headed writing paper survive. The business, T.J. Green and Thurstons Ltd, was established at Peckham Rye and Bermondsey. The business clearly survived the Second World War. From an invoice it seems that Tom also invested in a corset business after the first war. He must have been successful enough to enable him to invest in some properties in Peckham which in 1959 were put into a company, TJ Green Properties Ltd. There is a large tin box full of old title deeds relating to these properties.

In 1932 Tom bought a substantial semi-detached modern house near Dulwich Village, 95 Burbage Road. This is a far more salubrious part of London than the Old Kent Road. He paid £1625 for the property. He and Lizzie lived there until their deaths.

During the Second World War Tommy served in the Royal Air Force. I have not examined his service record, but there is a small suitcase with the papers and in it are the exercise books and training manuals for a flight mechanic and fitter. His service number and rank as a Leading Aircraftman are noted on a cover.

Neither Tommy or Eileen married and it seems they ran the business with their father.

In 1957 Lizzie died aged 67. The value of her estate is recorded as £2,550, a present day (2015) value of about £50,000. Tom survived her by ten years dying in 1967 aged 75. He had made a new will in 1958. His estate was valued at £36,753 – a present day value of about £590,000. The property company was put into liquidation but his estate took some time to wind up. The solicitor's final bill was not presented until 1970. In his will he left the Burbage Road house in equal shares to Tommy and Eileen *"in accordance with the wishes of their mother"*, and the residue as to three fifths to Tommy and two fifths to Eileen.

At some point thereafter Tommy and Eileen went to live in Broadstairs, Kent, though in separate houses. Tommy died in 1986 aged 71 leaving his entire estate to his sister, by then valued at £99,000 – present day value of £260,000. When Eileen died aged 90 in 2013 her estate was valued at £1,000,000. After some personal legacies and bequests to two animal charities and a cancer charity she left the bulk of her estate to her friend who was her next door neighbour. In her death certificate she is described as, 'a furniture retail store proprietor (retired)'.

There this particular branch of the Green family might have come to an end and been swiftly forgotten. But it was outside Eileen's house in Broadstairs that the skip stood and where Lizzie's letters were thrown, and afterwards discovered. I hope that her labour of love in penning her correspondence was not entirely in vain, and that in this way she can be brought to life again.

Appendix 1
Researched and contributed by
Graham Caldwell

GUNNER THOMAS JAMES GREEN
Service Record Transcription

TERRITORIAL FORCES
Army Veterinary Corps
Royal Field Artillery

ARMY VETERINARY CORPS
Home Theatre
1st London Division Veterinary Hospital, London WC
Later moved to Tunbridge Wells, Kent
Rank Private
Number 245, later changed to TT/0835
May 1916 to July 1917

- **5.5.1916:** Thomas Green is conscripted into the AVC (date Attested) rank Private, number 245 and is mobilised three days later to report for training at the 1st London Division Veterinary Hospital in London

W1. On this day Thomas signed the (by now) mandatory Territorial Force (TF) Imperial Service Obligation to serve overseas if required.

NB: Until 1916 the TF was lawfully recruited for home defence only and men could not be compelled to serve overseas unless they volunteered. This nicety was abolished in new legislation by the end of 1916.

- **Details taken from Attestation:** plus medical and other items in Thomas's file were recorded as follows:- Address: 74 Ossory Road, Old Kent Road, London SE; age 25 years + 6 months (elsewhere 'born 1890') occupation Salesman; height 5 ft. 5¼ inches; religion Church of England; next of kin Elizabeth Sophia Ann Green at the same address; children Thomas Leslie Green: born 28th May 1914 at 34 Darwin Street, Walworth, London SE and baptised on 9th June 1914 at St Mary's Church, Messenger St London SE by the Rev. Pitt.

- **8.5.1916**: Posted to 1st London Division Veterinary Hospital, 51 Calthorpes St, London WC. The 1st London (Territorial) Division was renumbered the 2/1st London Division in January 1916 and later renumbered the 58th Division, but paperwork was slow to adopt the new designations in the UK. By January 1916 the 58th Division's fighting elements

were transferred to France and after being
supplemented by in-theatre reinforcements remained
there for the remainder of the war, but its Veterinary
Hospital remained in England.

- **1.12.1916**: Thomas is transferred to the AVC of the
  regular army with new number TT/0835, but remains
  with the same hospital, which now moves to
  Tunbridge Wells in Kent.

- **26.12.1916**: Thomas is charged with AWL, being
  absent from midnight 26.12.16 to 27.12.16 and
  sentenced to 1 day's loss of pay. (Did he sneak home at
  Christmas to see the family?)

- **10.7.1917**: Thomas is transferred to the Royal Field
  Artillery, rank Gunner, number 245307.

ROYAL FIELD ARTILLERY

Rank Gunner
Number 245307, later changed to TF number 951761

**4th 'B' Reserve Brigade RFA, Bayton Camp
Worcestershire**
10th July to 7th October 1917
**1097th Battery, 216th (CCXVI) Brigade RFA 43rd
Division, Lucknow India**
8th October 1917 to 24th November 1919
Attached to 5th (Mhow) Division, Mhow India
August-November 1919

- **10.7.1917:** Posted to 4th 'B' Reserve Brigade RFA, Bayton Camp Worcestershire for training.

- **7.10.1917:** Embarked for India, posted to 1097th Battery, 216th (CCXVI) Bde RFA in 43rd (Wessex)

Division based in Bombay India on internal security
duties for the remainder of the war.

NB: The 43rd Division did not take part in any major
actions, but sent many drafts of infantry and artillery
formations to the Middle East during the war, but not
Thomas's artillery brigade (216).

- **20.4.1918**: Admitted to the British Station Hospital,
  Mhow, India, but condition not stated, but probably
  the same as for 3.4.1919 below. Prognosis "Satisfactory,
  no action taken" and released back to duty on 14.6.1918.

- **6.5.1919 to 8.8.1919**: The 1097th Battery took part in
  the Third Afghan War (6 May to 8 August 1919) which
  was a period prior to Thomas embarking for England
  in November 1919; however there is an explanation
  why he didn't leave with his unit, given below where
  his second hospital admission is documented.

- **3.4.1919**: Admitted to the British Station Hospital,
  Mhow suffering from Neurasthenia, an obsolete term
  used to describe a vague disorder "weakness of the
  actual nerves", but more commonly described today as
  chronic abnormal fatigability, moderate depression,
  inability to concentrate; loss of appetite, insomnia and
  other symptoms. Thomas was released to duty on
  26.6.1919.

- **22.8.1919**: Posted to the Royal Artillery Depot, Ambala, India; then later repatriated to the Office of ___? 5th (Mhow) Division for duty, based in Mhow. Mhow is in the Indore District of the Madhya Pradesh State.

- **2.11.1919**: Thomas appears for a second time on his Charge Sheet, but scant details given, other than the remark "Certified – no further action", which seems to indicate he was cleared of the charge.

- **24.11.1919**: Embarked Bombay for repatriation in England. The journey took until 15th December 1919.

- **16.12.1919**: Disembarked England.

- **21.1.1920**: Discharged "Surplus to Requirements" once the war was over, a common term used if not required to serve in the Army Reserve.

  WW1 SERVICE
  - Home 8.5.1916 to 6.10.1917
  - India 7.10.1917 to 22.11.1919
  - En Route UK 23.11.1919 to 15.12.1919
  - Home 16.12.1919 to 21.1.1920

Total Service: 3 years + 250 days

- **Post War:** Thomas's medical file is marked that he was discharged because he was suffering from gastritis and neurasthenia and was deemed to be 5% disabled, but not due to war service; nevertheless he was granted a pension from 13 January 1920 of 5/6d pw, plus 1/4d pw for his child. This seems to have been withdrawn in February 1920 if the code Z21 on his pension file refers to the payments authorised.

Award of the British Service Medal

- **12.2.1920:** Thomas's Discharge Certificate states "(Campaign) Medals Authorised Prior to 11th November 1918 NIL", despite it saying underneath "Has served overseas on active service". The **British War Medal** was instituted on 26th July 1919 and its official criteria for the army read as follows…

Officers and men of the British Army, including Dominion and Colonial forces, were required to have either entered an active theatre of war or to have left the United Kingdom for service overseas between 5 August 1914 and 11 November 1918, and to have completed 28 days mobilized service. The medal was also awarded in the event of death on active service before the completion of the prescribed period. The same criteria for eligibility were applied to members of the Women's Auxiliary Forces and staff of officially military hospitals and members of recognised organisations such as

the British Red Cross and the Order of Saint John who
actually tended the sick and wounded.

The segment highlighted in red would apply to those
serving in non-war zones, such as India, when the BWM
would be issued singularly (i.e. without the usual
accompaniment of the Victory medal).

Nevertheless on Thomas's 'Military History Sheet'
(undated and with the soldier's name left blank, but with
Lizzie's name and address at the bottom and the overseas
service dates matching exactly) under 'Campaign Medals
& Decorations' it clearly states British War Medal. Maybe
Thomas appealed?

- **1.3.1921**: On the RFA Medal Roll for the British War
  Medal, Gunner Thomas James name (number 951761,
  with "Previously 245307"also noted) is clearly listed
  as being in receipt of his campaign medal.

The British War Medal

Appendix 2

Photographs

Lizzie

Tom

Their Marriage Certificate

Ossory Road in 1977 before demolition. No 74 was identical to one of the terraced houses in the photograph

Army Form E. 624.

IMPERIAL AND GENERAL SERVICE OBLIGATION.

Agreement to be made by an officer or man of the Territorial Force to subject himself to liability to serve in any place outside the United Kingdom during the present period of embodiment.

I (No.) _2455_ (Rank) _Pte._

(Name) _Green. Thomas James._ do hereby agree to accept liability, during the present period of embodiment, to serve in any place outside the United Kingdom, in accordance with the provisions of Section XIII. (2) (a) of the Territorial and Reserve Forces Act, 1907, [and where, with a view to service overseas, my transfer to another corps is required, I hereby consent t such transfer notwithstanding that the corps to which I am to be transferred may be different from that in which I am serving].* I understand that release from this obligation can during the present period of embodiment be granted only with the consent of the competent military authority.

This undertaking is given on the understanding that I shall not by reason of such transfer suffer any reduction of the pay and allowances of which I was in receipt immediately prior to transfer.

T. J. Green (Signature of officer or man.)

_Ru___ (Signature of Commanding Officer.)
O. C. Administration Corp.,
L.M.B.A.S.C.

(Station) _51 Galthorpe Street Calthorpe St, W.C._

(Date) _5 May 1916_

* In the case of an officer the words in brackets should be omitted.

W 5353—1782 500,000 6/16 J. J. K. & Co. Ltd. Enc./Forms/E. 624/3

Tom's actual signed Imperial Service Obligation. This document released Tom for Home Defence duties with the Army Veterinary Corps and by it he volunteered for service overseas with any regiment the authorities thought fit.

TERRITORIAL FORCE.

4 years' Service in the United Kingdom.

Army Form E. 501.

ATTESTATION OF

No. 2—5 Name Green, Thomas James Corps Army Veterinary

Questions to be put to the Recruit before Enlistment.

1 What is your Name and Address?

1. 7th Osney Road
Old Kent Road

2. Are you willing to be attested for service in the Territorial Force for the term of 4 years (provided His Majesty should so long require your services) for the County of* to serve in the?

2. Period of service

3. Have you received a notice stating the liabilities you are incurring by enlisting, and do you understand them?

3.

4. Do you now belong to, or have you ever served in the Royal Navy, the Army, the Royal Marines, the Militia, the Special Reserve, the Territorial Force, the Imperial Yeomanry, the Volunteers, the Army Reserve, the Militia Reserve, or any Naval Reserve Force? If so, state which unit, and, if discharged, cause of discharge.

4.

5. Are you a British Subject?

5.

Under the provisions of Sections 13 and 99 of the Army Act, if a person knowingly makes a false answer to any question contained in the attestation paper, he renders himself liable to punishment.

I, Thomas ... do solemnly declare that the above answers made by me to the above questions are true, and that I am willing to fulfil the engagements made.

SIGNATURE OF RECRUIT.

Signature of Witness.

OATH TO BE TAKEN BY RECRUIT ON ATTESTATION.

I, Thomas ... swear by Almighty God, that I will be faithful and bear true Allegiance to His Majesty King George the Fifth, His Heirs, and Successors, and that I will, as in duty bound, honestly and faithfully defend His Majesty, His Heirs, and Successors, in Person, Crown, and Dignity against all enemies, according to the conditions of my service.

CERTIFICATE OF MAGISTRATE OR ATTESTING OFFICER.

I, Reginald White do hereby certify, that, in my presence, all the foregoing Questions were put to the Recruit above named, that the Answers written opposite to them are those which he gave to me, and that he has made and signed the Declaration, and taken the oath at 51 Walthampstreet on this day of

1916.

Signature of Justice of the Peace, Officer, or other person authorised to attest Recruits.

If any alteration is required on this page of the Attestation a Justice of the Peace should be requested to make it and initial the alteration under Section 80 [5], Army Act.
The Recruit should, if he receive a copy of the Attestation on Army Form E. 501A.
* Here insert County. † Here insert Corps.

0064

Tom's attestation

Believed to be Tom on horseback in India – a photograph to which reference is made in Lizzie's letters

London War Pensions Committee.

Replies to be
addressed to the
Honorary Secretary.

Telephone No.

Local Sub-Committee for..

Hop 292

Please quote reference

No. ....

17, Peckham Road,
Camberwell,
S.

24.3.19

Mrs Green

In re-assessing your case according
to instructions, you will be glad to hear
that your grant has been increased to at
the rate of 9/3 weekly from 4-3-19
Please let me know when your husband
is discharged.

Yours truly,

Dorothy M Whit.

Notification of Lizzie's improved grant after her interview

Rent book for 74 Ossory Road

Following Tom's return to England he starts the formalities before discharge

Serial No. *1.7.911.*   Army Form B. 2079.

NOTE—This Certificate is to be issued without any alterations in the manuscript.

Certificate of discharge of No. *245307* Rank *Gunner*

Name *Green* *Thomas James*

Surname.   Christian Names in full.

Unit*

and

Regiment or Corps } *R.H. & R.F.A.*

from which discharged

* The unit of the Regiment or Corps such as Field Co. R.E., H.T., or M.T., A.S.C., etc., is invariably to be stated.

Regiment or Corps to which first posted *Army Veterinary*

Also previously served in *N.Zl.*

Only Regiments or Corps in which the soldier served since August 4th, 1914, are to be stated. It inapplicable this space is to be ruled through in ink and initialled.

Specialist Qualifications (Military) *Nil*

CHEVRONS   *Three blue*

Medals, Clasps, *Authorized prior to Nov. 11th,* 1918, Stripes* *Nil*

Decorations and   To be inserted in words.

Mentions in dispatches

Has served Overseas on Active Service†

Enlisted at *51 Colchester St, H.Q.* on *8th May* 1916.

*Each space is to be filled in and the word "nil" inserted where necessary.

†To be struck out in ink if not applicable.

He is discharged in consequence of *being*

Surplus to Military requirements, having suffered

impairment since entry into the Service, Para.392(XVIA)K.R.

after serving* *Three* years* *250* days with the Colours, and

* *Nil* years* *Nil* days in the   or   { Strike out

              Army Reserve   { whichever

              Territorial Force† { inapplicable.

*Each space is to be filled in and the word "nil" inserted where necessary; number of years to be written in words.

†Service with Territorial Force to be shown only in cases of soldiers serving on a T.F. attestation.

Date of discharge *12 January 1920*

H. Collins   Lieut.   Signature

           for COLONEL   and

           Officer i/c   Records.   Rank.

1/c R.H. & R.F.A. RECORDS,

R.H. & R.F.A. (T.F.)   CHARLTON, S.E.7 (Place).

Description of the above-named soldier when he left the Colours.

Year of Birth *1890*   Marks or Scars

Height ft in.

Complexion

Eyes   Hair

(31817.) Wt. W1912/PP1188. 760m. 5/18. S. & C. (E3287.)   [P.T.O.

Tom's discharge – 12th January 1920

The furniture business on the Old Kent Road

656 OLD KENT ROAD, S.E. 15

LONDON 192

M ....

Dr. to TRUESHAPE CORSET Co.,

(T. J. GREEN)

STAY AND CORSET MAKERS

TO THE TRADE.

Tom branches out with Lizzie after the war

T. J. GREEN & THURSTONS LTD.

CASH FURNISHERS, DRAPERS & GENERAL GOODS

HEAD OFFICE

816 & 818, OLD KENT ROAD, PECKHAM, S.E.15. NEW Cross 2660.

70, 70a & 72, PECKHAM RYE, S.E.15. NEW Cross 4005.

SOUTHWARK PARK ROAD, BERMONDSEY, S.E.16 BERmondsey 3333.

Registered Office : T. J. Green Properties Ltd.

The writing paper of the business after the Second World War

Feb 2nd   74 Ossory Rd
                          Old Kent Rd

Dear Old Tom
    Just a line in answer to
you letter, I received 4 letters
and a parcel which has got
all brass things in dear thay
are beauitful I like them
very much, thay have got here
in good condision the 1lb of
sugar as well better than the
other parcel came dear nothing
broke at all, and I am
very pleased that with them
dear, I say dear I should
like some more of that
brass I think they look

Typical letter from Lizzie

Feb 20th 74 Ossory Rd
     Old Kent Rd

Dearest
Just a line hoping you are
quite well as it leaves us both
at present, Well dear we
have been to the pictures this
afternoon and they were
very nice dear, I wonder
when you will be home to
take us there dear, Well
dear I have had such
a longing for you this
week I cannot understand
it, I felt I would do
any thing to be with

Another example